Test Yourself in

EVIDENCE
CIVIL PROCEDURE
CRIMINAL PROCEDURE
SENTENCING

Test Yourself in

EVIDENCE
CIVIL PROCEDURE
CRIMINAL PROCEDURE
SENTENCING

Fifth Edition

Inns of Court
School of Law

BLACKSTONE PRESS LIMITED

First published in Great Britain 1994 by Blackstone Press Limited,
Aldine Place, London W12 8AA. Telephone: 0181-740 2277

© Inns of Court School of Law, 1994

First edition, 1994
Second edition, 1995
Third edition, 1996
Fourth edition, 1997
Fifth edition, 1999

ISBN: 1 85431 944 2

British Library Cataloguing in Publication Data
A CIP catalogue record for this book is available from the British Library.

Typeset by Style Photosetting Limited, Mayfield, East Sussex
Printed by Ashford Colour Press, Gosport, Hampshire

All rights reserved. No part of this book may be reproduced or transmitted in any form or by any means, electronic or mechanical, including photocopying, recording, or any information storage or retrieval system without prior permission from the publisher.

CONTENTS

Foreword vii

Introduction 1

A. The purpose of the multiple choice tests — B. The nature and format of the MCTs — C. MCTs – Popular misconceptions — D. Advice on taking the tests

The Civil MCT 10

Civil litigation — Civil evidence

The Criminal MCT 49

Criminal litigation and sentencing — Criminal evidence

Appendix 1 — Answers to the Civil MCT 85

Appendix 2 — Answers to the Criminal MCT 86

Appendix 3 — Note-form Answers to the Civil MCT 87

Civil litigation — Civil evidence

Appendix 4 — Note-form Answers to the Criminal MCT 119

Criminal litigation and sentencing — Criminal evidence

Appendix 5 145

Civil litigation syllabus — Criminal litigation and sentencing syllabus — Evidence syllabus

Answer Sheets 150

FOREWORD

This book has been published in conjunction with the Inns of Court School of Law, which runs the Bar Vocational Course. The course, which was introduced in 1989, was specifically designed to equip students with the evidential and procedural knowledge and the practical skills they will need to start their professional careers. It is gratifying to find that the course has been greeted as a major step forward in legal vocational training, and that it has attracted so much interest, both at home and overseas.

This book has been prepared by senior teaching staff at the Inns of Court School of Law and its primary purpose is to meet the needs of students enrolled on the Bar Vocational Course for 'mock' Multiple Choice Tests (MCTs) in order to test themselves in the important subjects of Evidence, Civil Litigation, Criminal Litigation and Sentencing prior to the MCTs in these subjects conducted annually at the School. The MCTs are designed to test whether students have the sound working knowledge and comprehension of these subjects that they will need in pupillage and the early years of practice. Although produced for a specific course, the book should also be of enormous interest and use to all students who wish to test themselves in these subjects, and their tutors.

This publication is revised annually, to keep it up to date and to improve its content with the benefit of experience and comments made by its readers. Comments are always welcome and may be addressed either to the Principal or the Course Director at the Inns of Court School of Law.

The continuing enthusiasm of the staff of Blackstone Press Ltd and their efficiency in arranging the production and publication of this book is much appreciated.

The Hon. Mr Justice Hooper
Chairman of the Board of Governors
of the Inns of Court School of Law
January 1999

INTRODUCTION

**PLEASE DO NOT ATTEMPT, OR EVEN READ,
THE MULTIPLE CHOICE TEST QUESTIONS
CONTAINED IN THIS BOOK UNTIL YOU HAVE READ
THIS INTRODUCTION!**

A. THE PURPOSE OF THE MULTIPLE CHOICE TESTS

It must be rare, on opening a book and turning to its first page, to be greeted by a command, albeit a polite command. However, there is a very good reason for such a command: that if you do embark upon testing yourself before you have read the following few pages on (a) the purpose of the Multiple Choice Tests (MCTs) (b) the nature and format of the MCTs (c) popular misconceptions and (d) advice on taking the tests, then it is likely that you will simply defeat the purposes of this book.

The MCTs contained in this book have two purposes. The first is to enable you to test, with speed and accuracy, whether you have a sound working knowledge and comprehension of the main principles of law and procedure, and the leading cases, in Evidence, Civil Litigation, Criminal Litigation and Sentencing. The MCT questions used are directed at the general rules, the principal exceptions to those rules and the leading authorities. Wherever possible, they concentrate on the modern law and important decisions. They are not directed at narrow, antiquated, abstruse or esoteric points that a practitioner, or even a scholar, might properly need to look up. This explains why, as we shall see, each question has to be answered in just over 2 minutes and 34 seconds.

The second purpose is to enable you, after the test, to identify, with precision, your weaknesses, the gaps in your knowledge and understanding, so that you can revisit these areas and take appropriate remedial action.

B. THE NATURE AND FORMAT OF THE MCTs

This book contains two MCTs, the Civil MCT and the Criminal MCT. In terms of style and difficulty, they closely resemble the MCTs conducted annually on the Bar Vocational Course at the Inns of Court School of Law.

Each of the MCTs comprises 70 questions, to be taken at one sitting. The Civil MCT incorporates questions on the subjects normally found in the syllabuses for courses in Civil Procedure and Civil Evidence. The subjects in question are set out in Appendix 5. The Criminal MCT incorporates questions on the subjects normally found in the syllabuses for courses in Criminal Procedure, Sentencing and Criminal Evidence. These subjects are also set out in Appendix 5. Neither MCT should be attempted until you have completed your studies in all of the subjects in question.

The 70 questions of each MCT have to be answered in 3 hours. This means that if you divide the time equally between the questions you will have just over 2 minutes and 34 seconds to answer each question.

The MCTs use the following headings to identify the subject matter of the various questions: CIVIL LITIGATION, CIVIL EVIDENCE, CRIMINAL LITIGATION AND SENTENCING and CRIMINAL EVIDENCE. So, if you wish to complete only part or parts of the MCTS, e.g., the Civil Evidence questions only, you should recalculate the length of the test by reference to the number of questions you intend to attempt.

Format

The questions in the MCTs contained in this book are always accompanied by four possible answers: [A], [B], [C] and [D]. You are required to select just one answer, the one that you think is correct/the best. You should record the answers you select on a separate question sheet (detachable from the inside back cover of this book), by putting a pencil line through [A], [B], [C] or [D]. (Pencils allow you to use an eraser and change your mind!)

The questions often take the form of a factual problem and conclude with a specific question, such as 'On these facts, what is the most appropriate advice to give to the client?' or 'On these facts, which of the following orders is the judge most likely to make?'. Questions of this kind are designed to test whether you are able to recognise the law or procedure appropriate to the given facts and/or whether you are able to apply the law to the facts and thereby identify the correct outcome.

Other questions take the form of a number of legal propositions, only one of which is correct or, as the case may be, incorrect, or ask about a specific point of law. Thus as to the former, the question may read, 'Which of the following propositions is correct?' or 'Which of the following propositions is INCORRECT?'. As to the latter, the question may state a rule of law and then conclude, for example, 'Which of the following is NOT an exception to this general rule?'. Questions of this kind are designed to test your knowledge of the law.

Some questions combine both a factual scenario and a choice of legal propositions so that, after setting out the facts, the question may read, for example, 'Which of the following best describes the principles which the Court should apply to these facts?'.

Creation & Validation

The questions used in the MCTs in this book are of the same kind and of the same standard as those used for assessment on the Bar Vocational Course; indeed, apart from the Civil Litigation questions, which test knowledge and comprehension of the new Civil Procedure Rules (and accompanying Practice Directions), the vast majority of the questions in this book were originally created for and have in fact been used for assessment on the course. The misperception, on the part of some students, that the questions in this book are easier than those used on the course, seems to stem from a failure to take the **Advice on Taking the Tests** proffered in this Introduction (see under **D.** below), in particular the advice to take the tests under examination conditions (which include a strict time limit and a ban on the use of books and other materials).

A lot of effort properly goes into the creation and validation of questions devised for use at the Inns of Court School of Law. Each question is thoroughly scrutinised by senior members of staff specialising in the subject in question and specialist practitioners.

Every effort is made to ensure that each question is clear, unambiguous and fair, with only one correct answer and three incorrect answers.

After each MCT, the results are then subjected to an item-by-item statistical analysis, to show the facility, selectivity and reliability of each question. Facility simply means the proportion of candidates who answered a question correctly – it indicates how easy or difficult a particular question was. Selectivity is a measure of the correlation between those who answer a particular question correctly and those who do well in the test overall. A high selectivity rating shows that most 'good' candidates have answered the question correctly. Reliability is a measure of the overall effectiveness of the question, the product of facility and selectivity. If there is an average facility and a high selectivity, the question is very reliable at differentiating between 'good' and 'bad' candidates.

Using this statistical information, it is possible to review, and if necessary amend, questions. For example, it may be desirable to amend or delete a question with an unduly high or low facility rating. Equally, in the case of a question with an unduly low selectivity or reliability rating, it is important to revisit the question to see whether it contained some ambiguity or was otherwise misleading, which might explain why 'good' candidates were getting it wrong.

C. MCTs — POPULAR MISCONCEPTIONS

'MCTs are easier than traditional examinations'

This view tends to be expressed by those who have never sat an MCT. By contrast, the experience of students who have taken MCTs, both at home and overseas, is that such tests are much more demanding than traditional examinations. There are three principal reasons for this.

First, MCTs allow examiners to cover the whole syllabus. For students who have been brought up on conventional examinations and who have adopted the 'question-spotting' approach, the MCT obviously comes as a very nasty shock!

Second, the MCT offers no scope for the candidate who would waffle. In conventional examinations, some students, unaware or not too sure of the correct answers, will hedge their bets, setting out at length all such seemingly relevant legal knowledge as they possess, but making no real effort to apply the law, simply skirting around the central issues with deliberate equivocation. There is no scope for such tactics in the MCT: faced with 4 competing answers, only one of which is correct, you must nail your colours to the mast.

Third, there is the obvious pressure that comes from having to answer 70 questions at the rate of about 2½ minutes per question. This calls for the ability to analyse, digest and comprehend material at speed, before reaching a firm conclusion, only to move on to repeat the exercise in the next question, and so on.

'MCT means multiple guess or passing by good luck'

It is perfectly accurate to say that if you go into the examination room with no relevant knowledge at all and sit an MCT in which each question has four competing answers, then by the law of averages you *could* score 25%. However, the pass-mark is usually more than double 25%. On the Bar Vocational Course, for example, a student who answers correctly 60% of all the questions set, will achieve a bare pass; and in many jurisdictions the percentage required to pass is much higher. Students relying on guesswork or Lady Luck simply do not pass. However, as will be stressed below, when you do not know, or are unsure about, the correct answer to a particular question, you *should* make an intelligent guess, because no mark is deducted for a wrong answer.

'MCTs are inferior to traditional tests and examinations'

The validity of this criticism depends upon what one is seeking to test or examine. Obviously the MCT is not an appropriate tool to test oral legal skills such as Advocacy or Negotiation, just as it would be an inappropriate means of testing the practical skills of a pianist or an airline pilot. Equally, it cannot test a student's *written* skills, whether in drafting a pleading, writing a legal essay or answering a legal problem (although it is interesting to note, in passing, that there is a high degree of correlation between student results in MCTs and in other forms of testing which do involve oral performances and written work). However, experience shows that the MCT is an excellent vehicle for testing, with accuracy, reading ability, powers of analysis, and levels of knowledge and comprehension. MCTs have been used to test doctors at both undergraduate and postgraduate level, and in other disciplines, for many years. Moreover, there is no question of examiner bias.

'MCTs cannot test the "grey areas"'

This is simply incorrect! For every 'grey area' question, there can be a suitably 'grey area' answer. For example, if on a particular point the authorities conflict, the correct answer may simply read, 'The authorities are in conflict on this point'. (Note, however, that such wording may also be used for an incorrect answer, i.e., in a question on a point on which the authorities are not in conflict at all.) Another possibility, in 'grey areas', is to build a question around the facts of an important reported case, thereby testing whether a student knows of, and has understood, that case. That said, it is certainly true that it can be more demanding to set good MCT questions on 'grey areas', and for this reason they tend to be avoided, unless they concern important areas of the law.

D. ADVICE ON TAKING THE TESTS

The purpose of the MCTs in this book is likely to be defeated unless you observe certain basic rules.

1. DO NOT ATTEMPT AN MCT UNTIL YOU HAVE COMPLETED YOUR STUDIES IN THE SUBJECTS COVERED

The MCTs in this book are designed to be taken only *after* you have completed your studies in the subject areas covered and *before* you are formally examined in them.

2. TAKE THE MCT UNDER EXAMINATION CONDITIONS

Make sure that you will have an *uninterrupted* period of 3 hours in which to complete the *whole test*. If you wish to complete only part or parts of either MCT, for example the Evidence questions only, you should recalculate the length of the test by reference to the number of questions you intend to attempt and the number of permitted minutes per question (roughly 2 minutes and 34 seconds). If you are working at home, tell the other residents that you do not wish to be disturbed, and take the telephone off the hook! Also remove from the room any relevant books or materials that you might be tempted to use – the MCT is a closed-book examination.

3. USE THE ANSWER SHEET

On starting the test, detach the appropriate Answer Sheet from the inside back cover of this book and read carefully the Instructions on that Answer Sheet.

4. OBSERVE THE TIME LIMITS

Observe the overall time limit (if necessary by using an alarm clock) and try to spend no longer than an average of about $2\frac{1}{2}$ minutes on each question. You will doubtless find that some of the questions can be answered in less time, whereas others require slightly more time – the questions vary in length and difficulty. However, the overall time limit reflects the standard of the MCT as a whole, and should not be exceeded.

5. READ ALL FOUR COMPETING ANSWERS TO EACH QUESTION BEFORE MAKING A SELECTION

Whether a problem-type question or a propositions-type question, you should *always* look at all four competing answers before making a selection. There are three good reasons for doing so.

First, an answer may refer to another answer or answers. For example, the question may set out a judge's ruling on a particular point of law, and conclude, 'Which of the following reasons could justify the judge's ruling?'. [A] may then set out one reason and suggest that this *alone* could justify the ruling; [B] may set out a different reason and suggest that this *alone* could justify the ruling; and [C] may read, 'The reasons in both [A] and [B]'.

Second, even when you are relatively confident that you know the correct answer before you even look at the options on offer, and you are therefore tempted to simply select the 'correct' answer and to ignore the other answers, reading those other answers to check that they are indeed incorrect is the best way of confirming your initial selection.

Third, there may well be occasions when you are unsure as to the correct answer. In these circumstances, it is often possible to identify the correct answer by the process of eliminating others which you know to be incorrect. Often you will find that the question-setter has included one answer which is quite obviously incorrect and another which is also incorrect, although not quite so obviously, thereby reducing the effective choice from four to two – the two remaining answers will test whether you have understood the legal principle in question.

6. TREAT THE EXAMINERS AS IF INFALLIBLE

If your initial reaction, on reading a particular question and the four competing answers, is that you need more factual information before you can select the correct answer, or that there are two correct answers, or that the correct answer seems to have been omitted, quickly swallow your pride and re-read the question to see if there is something which you have missed or the importance of which you failed to take note on the first reading. If, having re-read the question and answers, you remain convinced that you need more information, or that there are two correct answers, or no correct answer, then select the answer which, in your opinion, gets nearest to being correct or is the best from which you have to make a choice. Remember that most of the questions have been thoroughly scrutinised by specialist academics and practitioners and statistically tested in terms of their selectivity and reliability (see above).

7. IF NECESSARY, MAKE AN INTELLIGENT GUESS

As already explained, multiple choice does not mean multiple guess or passing by good luck. However if, having read a particular question, you do not know the correct answer and are unable to eliminate all of the incorrect answers, then you *should* make an intelligent guess, and move on. As we shall see, you do *not* lose a mark for a wrong answer.

8. MARK YOUR PERFORMANCE

After you have completed the MCT – and probably after a break of suitable length – you will want to mark your performance. You will find the correct answers to the Civil MCT and the Criminal MCT listed in Appendix 1 and Appendix 2 respectively. Award yourself one mark for each question that you have answered correctly. If you have selected one of the other three answers to the question, selected more than one answer, or not made a selection at all, you should *not* subtract a mark – you simply gain no mark for that question. You may then rate your overall performance according to the following table.

MCTs		Comment
Number of questions answered correctly	0–41	A performance ranging from the awful to the weak. At best, on 41, you are showing insufficient knowledge and comprehension in over 41% of all subjects tested.
	42–51	A performance ranging from one of bare competence to competence. You are showing insufficient knowledge and comprehension in c. 27–40% of all subjects tested.
	52–61	A performance ranging from the very competent to the all but outstanding. You are showing insufficient knowledge and comprehension in c. 13–26% of all subjects tested.
	62–70	An outstanding performance. You are showing insufficient knowledge and comprehension in less than 12% of all subjects tested.

9. REVIEW YOUR PERFORMANCE

After you have marked your performance, take a break! You need to be fully refreshed before you embark upon the most important part of the exercise, namely the review of your performance by reference to the note-form answers to the questions of the Civil MCT and the Criminal MCT, which you will find in Appendix 3 and Appendix 4 respectively. Thorough review is important because it allows you to identify with precision the gaps in your knowledge and understanding of the law with a view to further work or revision.

Look at *all* of the note-form answers, not just those to the questions which you got wrong. By looking at the answers to the questions which you answered correctly, you will usually confirm your understanding of the law. Sometimes, however, you may discover that although your answer was in fact correct, your reasoning was defective. Equally, you need to know the reasons for the answers as to which you could only make an inspired guess.

THE CIVIL MCT

[TIME LIMIT: 3 HOURS]

CIVIL LITIGATION

1. The Court of Appeal in *Anton Piller KG* v *Manufacturing Processes Ltd* (1976) laid down a number of pre-conditions for the making of an *Anton Piller* order (also known as a search order). Three of the four following propositions accurately reflect conditions stated by the Court of Appeal. One does not. Which one?

[A] There must be clear evidence that the defendants have in their possession incriminating documents or things, and that there is a real possibility that they may destroy such material before any application on notice can be made.
[B] The damage, actual or potential, must be very serious for the claimant.
[C] The claim must concern the infringement of intellectual property rights.
[D] The claimant must show an extremely strong prima facie case on the merits.

2. Julia issued a claim form not indorsed with her particulars of claim in the High Court against Rick alleging breach of contract. The only remedy she seeks is specific performance of the contract. More than a month has passed since the claim form was served and neither party has done anything since then. Julia wants advice about entering judgment in default at this stage. Which one of the following propositions is correct?

[A] Judgment in default is not possible because Julia's claim is for equitable relief which falls outside the rules allowing the entry of judgment in default.
[B] Judgment in default is not possible because Julia's claim for specific performance should have been commenced by a Part 8 claim, to which the default procedure does not apply.
[C] Judgment in default can be entered because the time for acknowledging service has expired and Rick has not returned the acknowledgment of service form.
[D] Judgment in default of notice of intention to defend cannot be entered at this stage because Julia has not served her particulars of claim.

3. Rachel wishes to commence proceedings to claim the cost of repairs to her car in the sum of £2,200 and compensation for minor bruising sustained in a road accident. Your instructing solicitor has asked for your advice on the nature of the proceedings if they are contested by the defendant. Which one of the following is the advice you should give?

[A] The action is likely to be a High Court small claims track case.
[B] The action is likely to be a County Court small claims track case.
[C] The action is likely to be a High Court fast track case.
[D] The action is likely to be a County Court fast track case.

4. Eric builds a house for Kate. The house is defective. Kate sues Eric in the High Court. Eric says that the fault was due to bad workmanship by George, one of his sub-contractors. Eric also claims that George damaged some of his equipment. Eric issues a Part 20 claim (third party notice) against George claiming an indemnity in respect of any damages awarded against him together with damages for the damaged equipment. Kate's action against Eric is struck out for breach of an 'unless' order. Which one of the following statements is correct?

[A] Both of Eric's claims against George fall with Kate's claim against Eric, and so Eric will have to issue a claim against George.
[B] Both of Eric's claims against George continue together as an independent action.
[C] Eric's claim for an indemnity falls with Kate's claim, but his claim for damages continues as an independent action.
[D] Both of Eric's claims against George continue, but the court will order separate trials because the relief claimed is not of the same or a similar nature.

5. Marine Fish Ltd, a large trawler concern operating around Dover, has suffered severe losses due, it says, to the dumping of phosphates off the French coast by the large French soap powder producers, Savon SA. Assume that there is a good cause of action against the defendant, that the tort was committed in France and that Marine Fish Ltd suffered damage in England. Marine Fish Ltd wish to know whether it can pursue a claim against Savon SA within the jurisdiction.

Which one of the following statements is correct?

[A] Since Savon SA is domiciled in France, a contracting state to the Brussels Convention, the claim must be pursued in France.
[B] Since the tort was committed on French territory, the claim must be pursued in France.
[C] Since the damage was sustained in England, Marine Fish Ltd should seek permission to serve the claim out of the jurisdiction under RSC O. 11.
[D] Since the damage was sustained in England, Marine Fish Ltd can sue Savon SA in France or in England. The choice is with Marine Fish Ltd. If it chooses to sue within the jurisdiction no permission is required to serve the claim.

6. You are instructed on behalf of Howard, who has been served with a claim form and an interim injunction made without notice restraining him from publishing an allegedly defamatory article about Agnes.

Howard has served a witness statement asserting that the contents of the draft article are true, and has applied to discharge the injunction. Which one of the following propositions best describes the principle that will be applied on the application?

[A] Provided there is a serious issue on the question of defamation, the court will consider the adequacy of damages to either side and the balance of convenience.

[B] As Howard has stated in his witness statement that he intends to plead justification, the injunction should ordinarily be discharged to protect freedom of speech unless the alleged libel is obviously untrue.

[C] As Howard has stated in his witness statement that he intends to plead justification, the injunction will be discharged to protect freedom of speech, and the court will not investigate the veracity of what Howard says in his witness statement.

[D] As the application is likely finally to dispose of the dispute, the injunction will be continued only if the merits of Agnes's case are overwhelming.

7. Robert moored his yacht 'Swift' alongside a quay at 7.30 am in a small North Wales village. When he reached the top of the steps he noticed an artist painting the harbour. He then set out for the nearby town with Miles, his crewman, for stores. On their return at 11 am they were aghast to find the 'Swift' severely damaged after a collision. There were, when they returned, several fairly large fishing vessels in the harbour which had not been there at 7.30. The artist was still painting. When Robert asked if he had seen what happened, the artist said that it was against his principles to tell tales on anyone. At the post office Robert found out that the artist was Vincent Morgan, and that he lived in the village. No one else seems to have seen anything. You are instructed to advise Robert.

Which one of the following is the most appropriate advice to give him?

[A] That a pre-action application notice be issued against Vincent requesting disclosure pursuant to the Supreme Court Act 1981, s. 33(2).
[B] That a claim be issued seeking a *Norwich Pharmacal* order against Vincent.
[C] That no pre-action disclosure is available against Vincent because he is protected by the privilege against self-incrimination.
[D] That no pre-action disclosure is available against Vincent because he is a mere witness.

8. David, a tenant, made out a cheque for £6,000 in favour of Peter, his landlord, in respect of rent due. On presentation, the cheque was dishonoured and accordingly Peter issued a County Court claim against David with Particulars of Claim claiming £6,000 due on the cheque. David has filed a defence and counterclaimed for damages of £4,000 for breach by Peter of a covenant in the lease to carry out certain repairs to the rented property (which has diminished the rental value of the property). Peter has now applied for summary judgment under CPR Part 24.

Which one of the following orders is the District Judge most likely to make?

- [A] Dismissal of the application.
- [B] Judgment for Peter in the sum of £6,000.
- [C] Judgment for Peter limited to the sum of £2,000 with the application refused as to the remainder of Peter's claim (i.e., £4,000).
- [D] Judgment for Peter in the sum of £6,000 but with a stay of execution in respect of £4,000 of the said £6,000 pending the trial of the counterclaim.

9. Isaac is claiming damages from his employer, Highbury Upholstery Ltd, in respect of a respiratory disease he alleges he contracted from involuntary inhalation of products used in the factory where he works. Eighteen months ago Isaac made an application to the Department of Social Security (DSS) for industrial disablement benefit. This involved completing an application form and attending a medical board, which completed a written report form. Highbury intend to apply for disclosure of these documents from the DSS.

Which one of the following propositions is correct?

[A] Highbury can only obtain an order for disclosure against the DSS after proceedings are commenced, the order being sought by application notice.
[B] Highbury can only obtain an order for disclosure against the DSS after proceedings are commenced, the order being sought by issuing a Part 8 claim.
[C] Highbury can first obtain an order for disclosure against the DSS before action, the order being sought by issuing a Part 8 claim.
[D] Highbury cannot obtain an order against the DSS for disclosure (other than by witness summons) because Isaac's claim is not for personal injuries.

10. Mark is injured in an accident at his place of work. He alleges that the machine in question was badly maintained and he believes that there have been similar accidents before. He brings County Court proceedings against his employer. In disclosure by lists, no mention is made in the employer's list of documents of accident reports relating to the earlier accidents involving the machinery. In these circumstances which one of the following is the application you would advise Mark to make?

[A] An order compelling the employer to attend before the District Judge for cross-examination as to the documents in his possession, custody or control.
[B] An order that the employer make a further and better list of documents.
[C] An order that the employer verify his list of documents by affidavit.
[D] An order for specific disclosure.

11. Which one of the following statements is correct?

[A] If a High Court claim is served outside the jurisdiction pursuant to the provisions of the Brussels Convention, judgment in default may be entered without permission once the extended period for acknowledging service has expired.
[B] Where there is an irregularity in a judgment entered in default, it will be set aside on an application by the defendant as of right.
[C] On an application to set aside a regular judgment entered in default, the primary consideration is the defendant's explanation for allowing the judgment to be entered.
[D] Judgment in default can be entered only when the defendant fails to acknowledge service within 14 days after the deemed date of service of the claim.

12. Where the court applies the guidelines in *American Cyanamid* v *Ethicon* (1975) on an application for an interim injunction, which one of the 4 following propositions best describes the degree to which the claimant must establish the merits of his case?

[A] The claimant must show that there is a serious issue to be tried.
[B] The claimant must show a strong prima facie case that his rights have been infringed.
[C] The claimant must show that his claim is more likely to succeed than fail at the trial.
[D] The claimant must show, on the balance of probabilities, that there is no defence to the action.

13. In proceedings brought by a Part 8 claim, when is the claimant required to serve his or her written evidence to be relied upon on the defendants?

[A] At the same time as the Part 8 claim form is served on each defendant.
[B] On each defendant within 14 days of that defendant acknowledging service.
[C] On each defendant at least 14 days before the day listed for the first Master's appointment.
[D] After the Master's appointment in accordance with directions made by the Master on that appointment.

14. Which one of the following propositions, all of which relate to applications for summary judgment in the High Court under CPR Part 24, is INCORRECT?

[A] Such an application can be made in any action in either the Queen's Bench Division or the Chancery Division subject to a limited number of exceptions.
[B] Such an application can be made for an injunction.
[C] Where a respondent to such an application intends to rely on evidence in opposition to the application, his evidence should be served on the applicant at least 7 clear days before the return day.
[D] Where a respondent to such an application pays money into court in compliance with a conditional order, such money remains part of the respondent's general assets if he subsequently goes bankrupt.

15. You have been asked to advise Dennis, who has been served with a claim form and particulars of claim seeking damages for breach of contract. Dennis does not accept that he was in breach, but has agreed with the view you expressed in conference that on the evidence there is a risk that he will be found liable. Your instructing solicitor is hopeful that proposals can be made which will lead to the claim being settled in the near future, but that it will be a few weeks before an offer can be made. Which one of the following is the best advice to give Dennis?

[A] Enter into negotiations with the claimant's solicitors, indicating in without prejudice correspondence that an offer to settle will be made in the next few weeks.
[B] File an acknowledgment of service, and then issue an application notice seeking an extension of time for filing the Defence.
[C] File a Defence, and ask for a stay for negotiation in the allocation questionnaire.
[D] File a Defence, and then issue an application notice seeking an order for a stay of the action to allow time for negotiations.

16. For some years James has purported to exercise a right of way along a path over Lynn's land. Hearing that Lynn intends to build an outbuilding across the path, James has applied on notice for an interim injunction. Which one of the following propositions best describes the relevance or otherwise of the fact that the building work has not yet commenced?

- **[A]** It has no direct relevance to the question whether the injunction should be granted, apart from being part of the factual background.
- **[B]** Its only relevance is as to whether damages would be an adequate remedy to either party.
- **[C]** It is likely to be the decisive factor if the other factors bearing on the convenience of granting the injunction are evenly balanced.
- **[D]** Its only relevance is in deciding whether the proposed injunction is mandatory or prohibitory.

17. Claude owns a large international pharmaceutical business of long standing based in Switzerland. Most of his trade is with the Far East, although he has a small number of dealings in England. Theresa has commenced County Court proceedings in London against Claude claiming £14,000 under a contract of sale governed by English law. A fully pleaded Defence was served 5 weeks ago alleging that the goods delivered were not of the required quality. Insurance monies in respect of another matter have recently become payable to Claude in London. One hour ago Claude received a telex in Switzerland to the effect that an order had been obtained by Theresa from Mr Justice Green restraining him from removing any of his assets from England, save in so far as they exceed £14,000, until judgment or further order. His London solicitors are now consulting you by telephone. Which one of the following is the best advice to give Claude?

- **[A]** To press the insurance company for payment before they are notified of the order.
- **[B]** To apply for the order to be discharged on the ground that, proceedings having been served, notice of the application to Mr Justice Green should have been given to Claude.
- **[C]** To apply for the order to be discharged on the ground that such an order cannot be made after service of a fully pleaded Defence.
- **[D]** To apply for the order to be discharged on the ground that Claude is not the sort of defendant against whom such an order should be made.

18. Richard, who owns a garden centre, purchased some catalogues from Barchester Printing Limited. The catalogues, which were supplied in September 1992, were very poorly printed. Richard served proceedings together with his particulars of claim in July 1998. In October 1998 Barchester served a Defence alleging that the contract was made not with it but with Barchester Printing (1982) Limited, a different company but with the same registered office. It is now March 1999 and Richard wishes to amend his proceedings by substituting Barchester Printing (1982) Limited for Barchester Printing Limited. Which one of the following correctly describes the principle that will be applied by the court?

[A] Richard's application may be granted if he can show he made a genuine mistake as to the name of the defendant and that his mistake was not misleading.
[B] Richard's application may be granted because the companies have the same registered office.
[C] Richard's application cannot be granted because the court has no jurisdiction to allow such an amendment once the limitation period has expired.
[D] Richard's application cannot be granted unless he can show that Barchester deliberately tried to mislead him as to the identity of the contracting party.

19. On an assessment of costs on the standard basis, which one of the following principles should be applied?

[A] There should be allowed all costs except in so far as they are of an unreasonable amount or have been unreasonably incurred, any doubts being resolved in favour of the receiving party.
[B] The court shall have an unfettered discretion as to the items of expenditure to be allowed and as to the amount to be allowed in respect of such items.
[C] The party paying the costs shall not be ordered to pay more than such amount (if any) as is reasonable having regard to the financial circumstances of all the parties and their conduct in connection with the dispute.
[D] There should be allowed a reasonable and proportionate amount in respect of all costs reasonably incurred, any doubts being resolved in favour of the paying party.

20. After judgment has been obtained in the High Court, which one of the following methods of enforcement is not executed by the sheriff?

[A] Seizure and sale of the judgment debtor's goods in satisfaction of a money judgment.
[B] Seizure of listed and identified goods for delivery to the claimant.
[C] Attaching a debt due from a third party to the judgment debtor so that the third party is required to pay the debt direct to the judgment creditor.
[D] Removal of persons from land and giving possession to the claimant.

21. In November 1995 your client Julia was injured at work through the negligence of her employers, Cannonfodder Ltd ('CF'), in circumstances where her cause of action accrued immediately. She consulted your instructing solicitors in May 1997. Proceedings were issued in the old format of a County Court summons against CF in October 1998. As negotiations had by then reached a sensitive stage, your instructing solicitors decided that service should be delayed pending the outcome of negotiations. They did not notify CF's solicitors that proceedings had been issued.

It is now May 1999, negotiations have broken down, and the summons has still not been served. CF's solicitors have indicated that CF will defend the action, inter alia on the grounds that it is now too late for Julia to serve the summons. You have advised Julia that the period of validity of the summons has expired. Which one of the following reflects the additional advice you should give Julia?

[A] As more than 4 months have elapsed since the summons was issued, it is now too late for the court to grant an extension to the period of its validity.
[B] That the summons will not be renewed, and the court has no power under the Limitation Act 1980, s. 33 on these facts to direct that the primary limitation period shall be disapplied.
[C] That there are strong grounds for seeking an order renewing the summons for a sufficient period to allow for service.
[D] That the summons cannot be renewed, but a second summons may be issued in respect of Julia's injuries, and an application under the Limitation Act 1980, s. 33 may be made with some prospects of success for a direction that the primary limitation period shall be disapplied.

22. Rupert brings High Court proceedings against Gaston claiming damages in respect of an alleged breach of contract made in England. Gaston has substantial assets in England, but is domiciled in Belgium. Belgium, like England and Wales, is a Brussels Convention country. Rupert wishes to obtain a *Mareva* injunction (also known as a freezing injunction) against Gaston. Which one of the following statements, regarding the power of the High Court to grant a *Mareva* injunction, is correct?

[A] A *Mareva* can never be granted against a defendant who is domiciled in another Convention country.
[B] It is irrelevant to the grant or refusal of a *Mareva* that the defendant is domiciled in another Convention country.
[C] A *Mareva* can only be granted against a defendant who is domiciled in another Convention country if a court possessing jurisdiction to grant that country's equivalent of a *Mareva* first gives its consent.
[D] The relative ease of enforcement of judgments against a defendant domiciled in another Convention country is a factor to be taken into account in deciding whether or not to grant a *Mareva*.

23. Magic Makeup Plc, an English company, contracted to buy a quantity of lipsticks from Daisy Bell Products Inc., an American company incorporated in New York. By its terms, English law is to govern the contract. The contract also contains a jurisdiction clause which states 'the High Court in London shall have jurisdiction to determine any disputes arising out of this contract'. Daisy Bell Inc. have considerable assets in England. Magic Makeup now want to sue Daisy Bell for breach of contract in the High Court in London. Magic Makeup should be advised:

[A] That the English courts have jurisdiction by virtue of the fact that the claimant (i.e. Magic Makeup) is incorporated in England.
[B] That Magic Makeup should seek permission from the High Court to issue and serve a claim on Daisy Bell in the USA.
[C] That Magic Makeup can serve a claim on Daisy Bell in the USA without permission.
[D] That Magic Makeup will have to sue Daisy Bell in New York, as, due to the fact that Daisy Bell are incorporated there, those courts have sole jurisdiction.

24. Winston is suing Laura for damages for an alleged breach of contract committed 3 years ago. Laura served Winston with a Request for Further Information of the Particulars of Claim 7 months ago, and the Master made an order 5 months ago requiring Winston to provide that Information within the next 21 days. Winston has not yet served the Information. Which one of the following orders is most likely to be made upon an application by Laura?

[A] An order with a sanction in default in respect of the Further Information.
[B] An order dismissing the action on the grounds of inordinate and inexcusable delay.
[C] An order striking out the Particulars of Claim as an abuse of the process of the court.
[D] An order that the action be discontinued.

25. Jane is suing her employer for damages following an accident when her arm was trapped in the doors of a lift at work. You are instructed to advise Jane whether it is possible to obtain copies of her employer's witnesses' statements before trial. Which one of the following correctly states the situation?

[A] There is jurisdiction to order the exchange of witnesses' statements only in the specialist courts, such as the Commercial and Admiralty Courts, of the High Court.
[B] Mutual exchange of witnesses' statements is one of the directions usually made at the allocation stage or case management conference in both the High Court and the County Court.
[C] Whether the action is proceeding in the High Court or the County Court, requiring an exchange of witnesses' statements is only possible if an order is made on an application to the court.
[D] Witnesses' statements are covered by legal professional privilege, and it is not possible to obtain an order for the disclosure of the other side's witnesses' statements.

26. A County Court Circuit Judge gives final judgment in the sum of £6,000 in an action based on an alleged breach of contract. If the defendant wishes to appeal, to which one of the following should the appeal be brought?

[A] The Divisional Court.
[B] A High Court Judge in private.
[C] A High Court Judge sitting in public.
[D] The Court of Appeal.

27. Paul has made a personal injuries claim which has been allocated to the multi-track. Last year he disclosed a report on his injuries by Mr Brown, a consultant surgeon. More recently Paul has decided to change experts, and earlier this year he disclosed a more favourable report by Mr Green. The case has now come on for trial. Mr Green has been called for Paul, but Mr Brown has not. Mr Brown's report corresponds with a report from Mr White prepared for the defendant. Paul objects to the defendant putting in evidence Mr Brown's report. How should the judge rule on the defendant's application to adduce Mr Brown's report?

[A] That it is inadmissible by virtue of the implied undertaking not to use the report without the consent of the party who disclosed it, in this case Paul.
[B] That it is inadmissible without Paul's consent by virtue of the confidential relationship between doctor and patient.
[C] That it is protected by legal professional privilege, unless Paul waives the privilege.
[D] That it is admissible regardless of Paul's consent.

28. You are instructed by Kurall plc, a company that manufactures drugs, against whom proceedings have been commenced in the High Court by Miss Sparrow. Miss Sparrow was diagnosed by her doctor to be suffering from a muscle virus. The doctor prescribed the use of Zendion Plus, one of the drugs manufactured by Kurall plc. He prescribed no other drugs to Miss Sparrow and explained to her that in no circumstances was she to take Zendion Plus in conjunction with any other medication. Miss Sparrow alleges that, far from curing her condition, Zendion Plus has made it worse. A medical report, prepared at the request of Kurall plc in contemplation of the litigation, concludes that 'it is almost certain that Miss Sparrow, at the time when she was taking Zendion Plus, was also taking other drugs, the nature of which, however, cannot be stated with accuracy'. Kurall plc wants to know how it may discover the nature of the other drugs used. Which one of the following courses of action would it be most appropriate to take?

[A] To apply for an order for specific disclosure.
[B] To apply under the Supreme Court Act 1981, s. 34(2) for an order for disclosure against a non-party to the proceedings.
[C] To serve a request for further information on Miss Sparrow.
[D] To rely upon the tactic of surprise by awaiting trial and then cross-examining Miss Sparrow about the other drugs used.

29. Immediately before the trial of an action commenced by Roger against William, the trial judge makes an order that a question be referred to the European Court. Which one of the following best describes the effect of such a reference?

[A] The English action will be stayed until the European Court has given a preliminary ruling on the referred question, and the English courts will be bound by that ruling on that question.
[B] The English trial will immediately proceed, and the trial judge will decide all issues apart from the question referred to the European Court. The action will then be adjourned until the European Court has given a ruling on the question, when judgment will be given by the English court.
[C] Roger and William will be required to agree the facts, which will be annexed to the reference to the European Court in a schedule, and the European Court will then give judgment to Roger or William in accordance with its decision on the question referred.
[D] The English action will be discontinued, and Roger will be required to commence a fresh action before the European Court, which will decide all the issues between the parties and give judgment accordingly.

30. Kate, who is making a claim for personal injuries, has made an application for an interim payment. The application was argued by counsel, and resulted in an interim payment of £4,000. The order made by the District Judge says nothing about costs. What does this mean?

[A] That the costs of the application form part of the general costs of the action.
[B] That the costs of the application will not be payable immediately, but will become payable after the final determination of the action.
[C] That no costs are payable in respect of the application.
[D] That the liability to pay the costs of the application will be left to be determined by the trial judge.

31. Which one of the following propositions concerning Notices to Admit Facts is INCORRECT?

[A] An admission made by a party in compliance with a Notice to Admit is made for the purposes of that claim only.
[B] An admission made by a party in compliance with a Notice to Admit may be withdrawn with the permission of the court.
[C] An admission made by a party in compliance with a Notice to Admit may not be used in favour of any person other than the person by whom the Notice was given.
[D] If a party fails to reply to a Notice to Admit facts he will be deemed to admit the facts stated in the Notice.

32. You have been briefed to attend a case management conference on behalf of the defendant in a contractual dispute. At the hearing the judge indicates a view of what he considers to be the only issues that ought to be tried, the issues identified by the judge being narrower than the issues raised by the parties' respective statements of case. Your opponent objects that the judge does not have power to narrow the issues in this way, and further indicates that he does not have instructions which will allow him to agree to the issues being narrowed in the way suggested by the judge. Which one of the following best describes the way the judge is most likely to deal with this situation in accordance with the rules?

[A] He should agree with your opponent, and leave the issues as they are.
[B] He is likely to adjourn the hearing to give your opponent an opportunity to get instructions on narrowing the issues.
[C] He is likely to adjourn the hearing to give your opponent an opportunity to get instructions, and is likely to make an order for the costs of the present hearing in favour of the defendant.
[D] He is likely to adjourn the hearing to give your opponent an opportunity to get instructions, coupled with a wasted costs order.

33. Fast Ltd have commenced a single action against Slow Ltd claiming damages for breach of contract in respect of allegedly defective building work and also for damages for late completion of the building works. Slow Ltd have paid £15,000 into court 'in satisfaction of all the causes of action in respect of which the claimant claims'. In these circumstances, which one of the following propositions is correct?

[A] When a payment into court is made where more than one cause of action is alleged, the defendant must allocate specific sums to each cause of action, so Slow Ltd's payment was irregular.

[B] Although Slow Ltd were entitled to make the payment in in the form they used, they can be asked to clarify how much of the payment relates to each cause of action, and the court may order them to clarify their payment notice.

[C] Slow Ltd had a choice as to whether to make the payment in in the form they used or by specifying individual sums for each cause of action, and Fast Ltd are not entitled to object to the form chosen.

[D] A payment into court must be in satisfaction of all the causes of action alleged in the proceedings, so Slow Ltd's payment was in the correct form.

34. On 27 February 1993, Duff Aluminium Co. Ltd ('Duff') delivered 30 tons of aluminium components to Peterborough Motor Manufacturing Plc ('Peterborough'). Peterborough paid Duff's invoice, but subsequently alleged that the components were too soft and useless. There has been voluminous correspondence between the parties, and solicitors have been instructed by both sides. Duff say that the soft aluminium identified by Peterborough must have come from another supplier. In December 1998 Peterborough's solicitors informed Duff's solicitors that a protective writ (the traditional means of commencing High Court proceedings, now replaced by the claim form) had been issued on 7 November 1998. In a letter dated 6 January 1999, marked 'without prejudice', Duff's solicitors replied:

> 'While it is denied that the soft aluminium came from our client, our client accepts there is a prospect of a court finding that in fact it did. We are at present seeking authority from our client as to proposals for settling this dispute, and would be grateful if you would consider postponing service for the time being so as to avoid unnecessary costs being incurred.'

It is now 31 March 1999. The writ has not been served, and the parties have been unable to agree terms despite a number of offers and counter-offers. Which one of the following is the best advice to give to Peterborough?

[A] Simply serving the expired writ and hoping Duff will not take the point that it is no longer valid is not an option, because the limitation period has expired.
[B] Although on the facts there may be a good reason for not having served the writ in time, any application to extend its period of validity will fail unless there is a satisfactory explanation for not making the application before the writ expired.
[C] As it is marked 'without prejudice', the letter of 6 January 1999 could not be referred to on any application to renew the writ. Therefore Peterborough could only point to continuing negotiations, so any application to extend the validity of the writ would fail.
[D] On the facts there is a good reason for not having served the writ in time, so an application to extend its period of validity should succeed.

35. William was employed by Domestic Chemicals plc. In April 1993 there was an escape of chemical vapours at the plant where William worked. In January 1994 William attended a routine medical examination, after which he was informed that as a result of the April accident, he had suffered latent damage to his lungs which would fully develop in about 2 years. In March 1996 William developed symptoms of bronchial asthma and had to retire. In October 1998 he sought advice from a solicitor, who told him that he had a good cause of action against Domestic Chemicals. Proceedings were issued and served in February 1999. You would advise Domestic Chemicals that the date when the limitation period started to run was:

[A] April 1993.
[B] January 1994.
[C] March 1996.
[D] October 1998.

36. Sally, who is in business buying and selling motor cars, has applied for summary judgment for the sum of £4,000, being the price of a motor car sold to Brian. In his evidence in reply to the application Brian sets out a long list of defects in the car and says he is refusing to pay on the ground that the car was not of satisfactory quality. Exhibited estimates put the cost of curing the defects at £2,500. If Sally does not contest the facts set out in Brian's evidence, which one of the following orders is the District Judge most likely to make?

[A] Dismissal of the application.
[B] A conditional order.
[C] Judgment for Sally in the sum of £1,500, dismissal of the application as to the balance.
[D] Judgment for Sally in the sum of £4,000 subject to a stay of execution in respect of £2,500.

37. April Fashions Ltd have served proceedings on Haymarket Insurance Plc claiming insurance monies alleged to be due under a policy after their premises were destroyed by fire. Haymarket have refused payment because they allege the fire was deliberately started by April Fashions' managing director. April Fashions' bank has foreclosed against the site of their former premises. Apart from the unpaid insurance monies April Fashions are clearly insolvent. On Haymarket's application for security for costs the Master considers that both sides have prospects of success at trial, but Haymarket's case is marginally stronger than that of April Fashions. How is the Master likely to deal with the application?

[A] He should disregard the merits of the case as they are not sufficiently overwhelming, and refuse the order because the defendants' refusal to pay on the policy contributed to April Fashions' financial problems, and to order them to provide security might stifle a genuine claim.

[B] Grant the order although April Fashions have an arguable claim, because the defendants are more likely to win at trial than April Fashions and April Fashions are clearly insolvent.

[C] Although he must always disregard the merits of the case, he should grant the order because April Fashions are clearly insolvent.

[D] Although he must take into account his finding that the defendants are more likely to win at trial than April Fashions, on balance he should refuse the order because the defendants' refusal to pay on the policy had contributed to April Fashions' financial problems and to order them to provide security might stifle a genuine claim.

38. You act for Laura, who is funding her case privately, and who is the claimant in a boundary dispute action against her neighbour, Martin, who is covered by a full legal aid certificate. At trial the County Court judge decides all issues in favour of Laura. What should you say to the judge on the question of costs?

[A] That in the circumstances Martin should be ordered to pay Laura's costs of the action, not to be enforced without the leave of the court.
[B] That as Martin is protected on costs by the legal aid certificate, there should be no order as to costs.
[C] That as all issues have been decided in favour of Laura, Martin should be ordered to pay Laura's costs of the action.
[D] That in the circumstances the question as to costs should be adjourned to allow the Legal Aid Board to intervene as you intend to apply for an order that the Legal Aid Board should pay Laura's costs of the action.

39. Which one of the following propositions concerning service and execution of *Anton Piller* (or 'search') orders is correct?

[A] Execution of an *Anton Piller* order must be supervised by a senior partner of the claimant's solicitors, who must be a person with experience of the operation of these orders.
[B] As a condition of the grant of an *Anton Piller* order the claimant undertakes to the court that the order will only be executed in the presence of the defendant's solicitors.
[C] The defendant must be informed of his or her right to obtain legal advice before complying with the *Anton Piller* order.
[D] An *Anton Piller* order can only be executed when the defendant's solicitors are present.

40. John sues Christopher for damage caused to his car during a 3-car collision with cars driven by Christopher and Mary. Christopher wishes to claim against Mary for the damage done to his own car and wishes to claim a contribution from Mary in case he is held liable to John. Christopher is unsure how he should make these claims against Mary. Which one of the following is the correct advice?

[A] He should issue and serve a Part 20 claim (third party notice) against Mary.
[B] He must issue separate proceedings against Mary.
[C] He only needs to write to Mary to inform her of the claims he has against her and the judge will do the rest at trial.
[D] He should serve a counterclaim against Mary.

CIVIL EVIDENCE

41. As a general rule, answers given by a witness under cross-examination to questions concerning collateral matters must be treated as final. Which of the following is NOT one of the exceptions to the rule?

[A] Where the witness denies bias towards the party on whose behalf the cross-examination is being conducted.
[B] Where the testimony of the witness is unfavourable to the case of the party calling him or her.
[C] Where the witness denies that he or she has any previous convictions.
[D] Where the witness denies that he or she suffers from some physical or mental disability that affects the reliability of his or her evidence.

42. Larry, a landlord, has brought an action against Teresa. He alleges that contrary to the terms of the lease, for three months (March, April and May) Teresa, his tenant, has failed to pay the rent and has not cleaned her windows at monthly intervals. In her defence, Teresa denies these allegations, claiming that (i) she paid the rent for March (ii) she cleaned the windows in March and (iii) at the end of March, she and Larry, by agreement, brought the tenancy to an end.

Who bears the legal burden on the following three facts in issue:

(1) non-payment of rent
(2) failure to clean the windows and
(3) termination of the tenancy by agreement?

[A] Larry bears the legal burden on (1), Teresa on both (2) and (3).
[B] Larry bears the legal burden on both (1) and (2), Teresa on (3).
[C] Larry bears the legal burden on (2), Teresa on both (1) and (3).
[D] Teresa bears the legal burden on (1), (2) and (3).

43. Marcus was injured during the course of his employment with 5-X Brewery Ltd, when the rung of a ladder on which he was required to stand when loading crates of lager collapsed, causing him to fall to the floor and damage his back. In his action for damages against his employers he alleged, inter alia, that his place of work was not kept safe. Section 29(1) of the Factories Act 1961 states 'every place at which any person has at any time to work . . . shall, so far as is reasonably practicable, be made and kept safe for any person working therein'. Who bears the evidential and legal burdens on the issue of whether it was 'reasonably practicable'?

[A] Marcus bears the evidential and legal burden.
[B] Marcus bears the legal burden; 5-X bear the evidential burden.
[C] 5-X bear the evidential and legal burden.
[D] 5-X bear the legal burden; Marcus bears the evidential burden.

44. Charles went on a world cruise lasting 9 months. He embarked on 1 January 1988. He was then aged 70 and in a state of poor health. In civil proceedings in 1996 the question arose whether Charles was dead. The court was satisfied, on the evidence, that since 1988 extensive enquiries had been made, and many advertisements had been placed, in various countries, by Charles' friends and relatives, but that no one had seen or heard from him since he embarked on the cruise. Under the presumption of death, what should the court have presumed?

[A] That Charles died on 1 January 1988.
[B] That Charles died on some day between 1 January 1988 and 1 January 1995.
[C] That Charles died on 1 January 1995.
[D] That Charles was dead.

45. Printers Inc., a publisher, bring an action against another publisher, M & N Ltd, for infringement of copyright. M & N Ltd admit that there are strong similarities between passages in one of their recent publications, 'Dieting Daily', and passages in a book, 'Daily Diets', in which Printers Inc. own the copyright, but allege that these similarities are purely coincidental. At the trial, Printers Inc. wish to adduce evidence of three other books published by M & N Ltd which bear strong similarities to books in which other publishing houses own the copyright. Should the trial judge admit or exclude the evidence?

[A] Exclude the evidence, because Printers Inc. have not alleged fraud or dishonesty.
[B] Exclude the evidence, because it is insufficiently relevant to the facts in issue.
[C] Admit the evidence, because of its relevance to the issue whether the similarities between 'Dieting Daily' and 'Daily Diets' are merely coincidental or due to copying.
[D] Admit the evidence, because of its relevance in showing that M & N Ltd have a disposition to commit conduct of the kind alleged.

46. Which of the following propositions concerning the law of evidence in CIVIL proceedings is INCORRECT?

[A] Questions relating to the law of any jurisdiction other than England and Wales are issues of fact to be decided, on the evidence given with respect to that law, by the judge.
[B] At common law a judge has no discretionary power to exclude evidence which is relevant and admissible as a matter of law on the ground that it may have been unlawfully obtained.
[C] Evidence of the character of a party or a witness is admissible only if it is among the facts in issue.
[D] The appropriate standard of proof in proceedings for committal to prison arising out of a civil contempt of court is proof beyond reasonable doubt.

47. During the course of the evidence-in-chief of Charles, a witness for the defendant, the trial judge grants leave to counsel for the defendant to treat Charles as a hostile witness. Counsel for the DEFENDANT now wishes to do the following:

(i) With the leave of the judge, prove that Charles has made a previous inconsistent statement (under the Criminal Procedure Act 1865, s. 3).
(ii) Ask Charles about a conviction which is recorded against him for perjury.
(iii) Adduce evidence to show that Charles is biased against the defendant.

Which of these, if any, should the judge permit?

[A] None of them.
[B] (i) but not (ii) or (iii).
[C] (i) and (ii) but not (iii).
[D] (ii) and (iii) but not (i).

48. John is suing ABC Ltd, claiming damages for breach of warranty, or alternatively for fraud. John took delivery of a boiler for his new restaurant. On the night he first opened the restaurant to the public, the boiler blew up and his specially invited guests were unable to dine. John alleges that one of the directors of ABC Ltd had represented to him that the boiler had been specially reconditioned and was as good as new, and that there was clearly a fraudulent misrepresentation because the director knew the boiler had not been reconditioned. What standard of proof is appropriate at the trial?

[A] On a balance of probabilities for breach of warranty and fraud.
[B] Beyond reasonable doubt for breach of warranty and fraud.
[C] On a balance of probabilities for the breach of warranty but beyond reasonable doubt for the fraud.
[D] Beyond reasonable doubt for the breach of warranty but on a balance of probabilities for the fraud.

49. Mary is bringing an action against her employers, Mane-Line Hairdressers, for damages for personal injuries sustained during the course of her employment as an apprentice. She claims that her scalp was burned and substantial quantities of her hair fell out when she was experimenting at the salon with some new permanent-wave lotion. In their defence, Mane-Line Hairdressers deny any liability and allege that Mary, having been instructed that apprentices were not to use any of the equipment without supervision, was acting in an unauthorised manner. This allegation is set out in Mane-Line Hairdressers' defence, and denied by Mary. If the matter comes to trial, how will the court regard this allegation?

[A] As a collateral matter.
[B] As a preliminary matter.
[C] As a fact in issue.
[D] As a fact of which the judge should take judicial notice.

50. Which of the following propositions is INCORRECT?

[A] A child may give unsworn evidence in civil proceedings.
[B] A spouse of a party to civil proceedings is competent to testify for that party.
[C] A spouse of a party to civil proceedings is not competent to testify against that party.
[D] It is possible for a competent and compellable witness in civil proceedings to refuse to answer specific questions on the grounds of privilege.

51. Which of the following presumptions is NOT capable of putting either a legal or evidential burden on the party against whom it operates?

[A] The presumption of legitimacy.
[B] The presumption of continuance of life.
[C] The presumption of formal validity of a marriage.
[D] The presumption of death.

52. Consider the following types of statement.

(i) A previous inconsistent statement made by a person called as a witness and proved, by virtue of s. 4 or s. 5 of the Criminal Procedure Act 1865, in cross-examination.
(ii) A previous statement made by a person called as a witness and proved for the purpose of rebutting a suggestion that that witness's evidence has been recently fabricated.
(iii) A statement in a document, made by a person called as a witness and used to refresh that witness's memory, which, by reason of cross-examination on the document, is made evidence in the proceedings.

In CIVIL proceedings, which of these statements is admissible as evidence of any fact stated therein?

[A] The statements in (i) and (ii) but not (iii).
[B] The statements in (ii) and (iii) but not (i).
[C] The statements in (i) and (iii) but not (ii).
[D] The statements in (i), (ii) and (iii).

53. The following statements all refer to the situation in which a witness under cross-examination has given an answer to a question on a collateral issue. Only one of the statements is correct. Which one?

[A] As a general rule, the cross-examining party is not permitted to call evidence designed to contradict the witness's answer.
[B] The tribunal of fact must accept the answer as final and therefore true.
[C] The cross-examining party is not permitted to ask any further questions about the issue or any other related issue.
[D] The answer will have no bearing on any of the issues to be decided by the tribunal of fact.

54. Philip is suing his employer for damages for negligence and breach of statutory duty arising out of an accident at work in which he was injured while operating a press. The employer is alleging contributory negligence. Immediately after the accident, Quentin, a fellow worker and witness to the accident, went to the foreman, Robert, and said that Philip had failed to follow the correct safety procedures before operating the press. Robert went to his supervisor, Sylvia, and told her what Quentin had said. Sylvia then went to the Safety Officer, Timothy, and told him what Quentin had said.

The employer wishes to rely on Quentin's oral statement for the truth of its contents. Assuming compliance with any relevant procedural requirements, which of the following best describes the manner in which that statement may be proved?

[A] By the evidence of Quentin (in which case, the statement shall not be given in evidence without the leave of the court).
[B] As in [A] or, if Quentin is not called, by the evidence of Robert.
[C] As in [A] or, if Quentin is not called, by the evidence of Robert or Sylvia.
[D] As in [A] or, if Quentin is not called, by the evidence of Robert, Sylvia or Timothy.

55. Beneficiaries bring an action against their trustee in the Chancery Division, alleging misuse of trust funds. The trustee is cross-examined as to the spending of the trust monies for his own purposes. He declines to answer, because his answer would incriminate him of the offence of theft.

Which of the following correctly describes the evidential position?

[A] He must not answer.
[B] He can refuse to answer and, if he does, cannot be liable for contempt of court.
[C] He must answer, but his answer cannot be used against him in the civil proceedings.
[D] He must answer, but his answer cannot be used against him should he subsequently be prosecuted for theft.

56. David, a pedestrian, is called on behalf of Euan in a negligence action brought by Euan to recover the cost of repairs to his car, which was involved in a collision with another car. David testifies that he saw both cars travelling at about 30 mph, that the defendant's vehicle was no more than 5 yards behind Euan's car, and that the defendant failed to stop in time when Euan had to brake suddenly at a zebra crossing. Although he has been a passenger in cars many times, David has never held a driver's licence. Is David's evidence admissible or inadmissible?

[A] Inadmissible because he is not qualified as an expert.
[B] Admissible non-expert opinion evidence.
[C] Inadmissible evidence of fact, i.e., evidence containing no statements of opinion.
[D] Inadmissible because it relates, in part, to the ultimate issues in the case.

57. One of the following statements relating to hearsay in civil proceedings is INCORRECT. Which one?

[A] Public documents are admissible as evidence of the facts stated in them.
[B] There are no statutory requirements as to how the court should estimate the weight (if any) to be given to hearsay evidence.
[C] A hearsay statement shall not be admitted if made by someone who at the time he made the statement was not competent as a witness.
[D] Where a hearsay statement is admitted in evidence and the maker of the statement is not called as a witness, evidence tending to prove that he made another statement inconsistent with it may be admitted.

58. In the course of a contractual dispute between Dick and Peter, Dick sent Peter a letter marked 'Private and Confidential' in which he disputed liability but offered Peter 50% of the amount he was claiming as due to him. Peter declined this offer and is now suing. Dick in his defence denies any liability. Peter would like to put Dick's letter in evidence. Dick objects. What should the judge's ruling be?

[A] That the letter is admissible against Dick because it was not marked 'without prejudice'.
[B] That the letter has no relevance to Dick's liability and is inadmissible for that reason.
[C] That the letter is inadmissible because it should be treated as if written without prejudice.
[D] That the letter is inadmissible because its prejudice is greater than its probative value.

59. Raymond is suing Steve for damages for injuries which Raymond suffered when their cars collided at a crossroads. Raymond alleges that Steve was negligent. Raymond will rely on the fact that Steve has been convicted by the local Magistrates' Court of driving carelessly at the time of their collision. Steve will deny negligence and claim that the conviction was erroneous.

On the issue of Steve's negligence, which one of the following statements best describes the legal position?

[A] Raymond must prove Steve's negligence.
[B] Raymond must prove Steve's negligence and will raise a rebuttable presumption of this by proving Steve's conviction.
[C] Whether Raymond proves Steve's conviction or not, Steve must prove he was not negligent.
[D] Raymond must prove Steve's negligence and will do so conclusively by proving Steve's conviction.

60. Jason, whilst receiving radiation treatment from some newly-installed equipment in an NHS hospital, was given a serious overdose. When Jason indicated that he would sue the hospital authority, the authority contacted the equipment manufacturers, who asked the authority for a report from the technician in charge. The technician supplied a report to the authority. They sent one copy to the manufacturers and another to their solicitors. Jason, who is now suing the hospital authority, wants to inspect the report, but the authority are claiming privilege for it, saying that one of its purposes was to get legal advice in case they were sued. Are they entitled to withhold the report?

[A] No, if the main purpose of the report was to find out what went wrong and to prevent it in future.
[B] No, because it was from the technician to his employers and therefore not a solicitor–client communication.
[C] Yes, irrespective of its purpose.
[D] Yes, if ordered to do so by the Minister of Health.

61. Imran is suing Denise.

At the disclosure stage, Denise's solicitor, Tom, inadvertently sent Imran's solicitor, Henry, a copy of a document for which legal professional privilege could properly have been claimed. When Tom realises his mistake and informs Denise, she makes a claim against Imran for delivery up of any copies of the document and for an injunction to restrain him from making any use of the information contained in them.

Which of the following best describes the test for deciding whether to uphold her claim?

[A] Whether the contents of the document are sufficiently relevant to the issues in the action.
[B] Whether the interests of Denise in keeping the information confidential outweigh the interests of Imran in seeking to make use of it.
[C] Whether a reasonable solicitor in the position of Henry would have realised that he had been permitted to see the document only by reason of an obvious mistake.
[D] Whether the document contains information which may enable Imran to advance his own case or to damage that of Denise, or which may fairly lead him to a train of inquiry which may have either of those consequences.

62. In a civil action by Philip against Denis arising out of the collision of 2 ships, both of which sank, aerial photographs taken of the 2 ships after the collision but before they sank have been admitted in evidence. Wendy, an expert in the field of maritime accident reconstruction, gives evidence that she examined the aerial photographs and consulted 2 articles (of which she is not the author) in a technical journal called 'Maritime Accident Reconstruction Monthly'. She also testifies that the journal is a source upon which maritime accident experts generally rely. Lastly she testifies that on the basis of her examination of the photographs, coupled with the information obtained from the articles, 'Denis's ship almost certainly crashed into the side of Philip's ship'. Assuming compliance with all relevant procedural requirements, was this evidence properly admitted?

[A] No, because it was evidence of opinion based in part on facts which were not within Wendy's personal knowledge.
[B] No, because it contained an opinion on the ultimate facts in issue in the case.
[C] No, because Wendy's evidence alone could not be used to establish that the journal is a source on which experts in this field generally rely.
[D] Yes.

63. Ms Militant, a civil servant in the Ministry of Agriculture, was expecting to be promoted but then found that a colleague, Placid, was promoted instead. Ms Militant suspects that she was passed over because she has been active in AGRO (her trade union) and/or because she is a woman. She is therefore bringing proceedings before an employment tribunal. She has asked the Ministry to disclose to the tribunal the personal file they have on her, and also that on Placid. The Ministry have refused on the ground that since the files contain information supplied in strict confidence they should not be disclosed in the interests of the proper functioning of the public service. How should the chairman of the tribunal rule?

[A] That he should inspect the files himself, and order discovery of one or both if he thinks it necessary.
[B] That the grounds relied on by the Ministry are valid and therefore they must withhold the files.
[C] That the Ministry must disclose to Ms Militant her own file, but must withhold Placid's file.
[D] That the Ministry may disclose or withhold one or both, at their discretion.

64. Farmer Dale entered into an agreement with Farmer Hill whereby Hill agreed to graze a flock of Dale's sheep on Hill's farm. Dale's sheep contracted a disease while on Hill's land and had to be destroyed. Dale claims the sheep were negligently kept on boggy land near a river rather than on Hill's drier grazing land. At the trial, a local farmer with a similar holding gives evidence that on the basis of his experience sheep should never be grazed on land of the kind in question because of the risk of contracting diseases. This farmer has been sheep farming for over 25 years, but has no formal qualifications. Assuming compliance with all relevant procedural requirements, was his evidence properly admitted?

[A] Yes, as expert testimony.
[B] No, because it is opinion evidence on matters requiring expert testimony but he is not an expert.
[C] No, because it raises collateral issues as to what another person has done on other occasions.
[D] Yes, as relevant factual, rather than opinion evidence.

65. Len was convicted of stealing certain items of jewellery. The jewellery was returned to the alleged owner Oswald. Len then commences a civil action for conversion against Oswald alleging that he (Len) is and always has been the owner of the jewellery. Oswald defends the action and wishes to introduce evidence of Len's conviction.

Which of the following best describes the legal position concerning evidence of the conviction?

[A] It is inadmissible.
[B] It is admissible but only on the issue of credibility.
[C] It is admissible and is conclusive evidence that Len stole the jewellery.
[D] It is admissible and creates a rebuttable presumption that Len stole the jewellery.

66. Tariq is suing Ursula. He wishes to introduce in evidence, for the truth of its contents, a written statement of opinion by Vera who is now living in Spain. The statement concerns a matter, which is highly relevant to the proceedings, on which Vera is not qualified to give expert evidence, but has been made as a way of conveying relevant facts that she personally perceived.

Assuming compliance with any relevant procedural requirements, may Tariq introduce Vera's statement in evidence?

[A] No, because it constitutes inadmissible opinion evidence.
[B] No, because it is inadmissible hearsay.
[C] Yes, but only with the leave of the court.
[D] Yes, and without the leave of the court.

67. Six months ago, Beatrice was arrested by PC Clout on a charge of supplying cocaine. At the trial, 3 months ago, she was acquitted. She has now commenced proceedings claiming damages for malicious prosecution. In the course of this civil trial, PC Clout, in his evidence-in-chief, testifies that he arrested Beatrice 'acting on information received in confidence'. In cross-examination, he is asked to name the source of the 'information received'. Should the judge allow PC Clout to answer this question?

[A] No, because the information was received in confidence.
[B] No, because it is in the public interest to protect the identity of informants.
[C] Yes, because disclosure of the name of the informant is necessary for Beatrice to establish her claim.
[D] Yes, but only if PC Clout is willing to answer it.

68. A national newspaper suggests that a new Bishop's appointment has been made on political grounds. The Bishop sues for libel. At the trial, the journalist who wrote the article gives evidence that the Bishop was appointed after making a large donation to the political party in power and after undertaking to support government policy when appointed. When asked to name the sources of his information the journalist refuses, saying that he has a privilege under the Contempt of Court Act 1981, s. 10. How should the judge rule?

[A] He has an absolute right to refuse to disclose his source.
[B] He need not answer unless it is 'necessary' in the interests of justice or national security or for the prevention of disorder or crime.
[C] He must not answer without his source's consent because the public interest requires free access to the media to expose official wrongdoing.
[D] He must answer.

69. Charles is suing Daniel for breach of contract. Charles, in the light of a statement made by Edward to his (Charles's) solicitors, calls Edward as a witness. Edward gives evidence which totally contradicts the statement, and the judge allows him to be treated as hostile.

Is the statement admissible?

[A] No, because hearsay.
[B] Yes, for the truth of its contents and to establish Edward's inconsistency.
[C] Yes, but *only* to establish Edward's inconsistency.
[D] No, because irrelevant.

70. Which of the following statements about the doctrine of judicial notice after enquiry is INCORRECT?

[A] The doctrine applies only to facts which are beyond serious dispute, notorious or of common knowledge.
[B] The doctrine allows the judge, before taking judicial notice, to consult sources such as authoritative works of reference and almanacs.
[C] Once the judge has taken judicial notice of a fact under the doctrine, then generally it will constitute a binding legal precedent.
[D] Under the doctrine, the rules of evidence do not apply to the enquiry undertaken by the judge.

THE CRIMINAL MCT

[TIME LIMIT: 3 HOURS]

CRIMINAL LITIGATION AND SENTENCING

1. You represent Samantha who consents to summary trial on a charge of receiving stolen goods. You intend to call Samantha herself and a character witness. You can:

[A] Make both an opening and a closing speech as of right.
[B] Make an opening speech, and then apply to the magistrates to allow you to make a closing speech as well.
[C] Make only a closing speech since the only witness whom you are calling other than the accused is not a witness of fact.
[D] Make only a closing speech since in a summary trial the defence cannot make an opening speech.

2. Gerald is arrested in connection with the murder of Harriet. He has been informed of his rights. He has now been lawfully detained for a period of 96 hours. The investigation is not yet complete, and the police wish to detain him for further questioning. In these circumstances, the investigating officers must:

[A] Take him before a Magistrates' Court who may authorise detention for a further 36 hours.
[B] Obtain authorisation from an officer of not less than the rank of superintendent, who may authorise detention for a further 6 hours.
[C] Release him or charge him.
[D] Release him on bail and then immediately re-arrest him for the murder of Harriet.

3. Here are 4 separate situations involving Mike (aged 15). In the first 3, he appears in court with Neville (aged 18). Only summary offences are involved. Mike and Neville always plead Not Guilty.

In which one of the following situations does the adult Magistrates' Court have NO discretion to send Mike to the Youth Court for trial?

[A] Neville appears in the Magistrates' Court with Mike. Mike is charged with driving whilst disqualified, Neville is charged with aiding and abetting him.
[B] Mike and Neville appear in the Magistrates' Court jointly charged with taking a car without the owner's consent.
[C] Mike and Neville appear in the Magistrates' Court on two separate charges. Neville is charged with common assault against Peter, and Mike is charged with common assault against Robert, the two assaults allegedly occurring during a brawl involving all four people.
[D] Mike appears alone in the Magistrates' Court to be tried on a charge of assaulting a police officer in the execution of his duty. The magistrates start the trial under the mistaken impression that Mike is 18 years old but then discover his true age.

4. Tom was charged with theft by the police. He was released on bail, the sole condition being that he surrender to custody at Ashbridge Magistrates' Court in 14 days' time.

Seven days after Tom's release, a police officer saw him at Ashbridge railway station. Tom was about to board a train and had a large suitcase in his hand. The officer, believing that Tom was going away and was unlikely to surrender to the court on the due date, arrested Tom.

Tom wants advice on whether the arrest at the railway station was lawful or not. Which one of the following statements is correct?

[A] The police officer had no power to arrest Tom. He should have applied immediately to a magistrate for a warrant to arrest Tom.
[B] The police officer had no power to arrest Tom. He should have waited to see if Tom attended court on the due date. If Tom had failed to attend court, a bench warrant for his arrest could then have been sought.
[C] The police officer had the power to arrest Tom provided that his belief that Tom would not surrender to custody at the court was a reasonable belief.
[D] The police officer had the power to arrest Tom because Tom had been charged with theft, which is an arrestable offence.

5. Daniel and Edward both appear in the Magistrates' Court. Daniel is charged with theft of a television set and Edward is charged, in a separate information, with dishonestly receiving the television set, knowing or believing it to be stolen. They do not wish to be tried together. Your advice to them should be that:

[A] As both offences arise out of the same incident, they will be tried together automatically.
[B] They cannot be tried together unless they both agree.
[C] As this is not a joint charge, there will automatically be separate trials.
[D] They will be tried together if the magistrates decide that the offences are so related to each other that a joint trial is necessary in the interests of justice.

6. Frank is charged with criminal damage and burglary. The facts alleged by the prosecution are that Frank broke a window, valued at £75 (the criminal damage) to gain access to property from which he stole various specified items (the burglary). In these circumstances:

[A] Frank may elect trial on indictment for the burglary, but the criminal damage must be tried summarily.
[B] Frank may elect trial on indictment for both offences.
[C] Frank has no right to elect trial on indictment.
[D] Frank may elect trial on indictment for the burglary, and the criminal damage may be included, by the prosecution, in the indictment.

7. Frank is committed to Barchester Crown Court to stand trial on a charge of burglary. He fails to attend court on the date fixed for his trial. He is charged with the offence of failing without reasonable cause to surrender to custody, under the Bail Act 1976, s. 6. Which one of the following statements about the Bail Act offence is correct?

[A] The offence should be dealt with at the Crown Court by a judge sitting alone.
[B] The offence should be dealt with at the Crown Court by a judge sitting with a jury.
[C] The offence should be dealt with at the Crown Court by a judge sitting with 2 magistrates.
[D] The offence is a purely summary one and so must be dealt with by the Magistrates' Court.

8. Alan was charged with assault occasioning actual bodily harm. He was not legally represented. When the charge was put to him in the Magistrates' Court, he said 'Guilty but I was acting in my own defence'. After hearing mitigation the magistrates proceeded to sentence him. Alan subsequently seeks advice on appeal. You should advise him that:

[A] He can appeal against conviction to the Crown Court which may quash the conviction and substitute an acquittal if it decides that the plea was equivocal.
[B] He can appeal against sentence only as he pleaded guilty.
[C] He can appeal against conviction to the Crown Court and that appeal will take the form of a retrial.
[D] He can appeal against conviction to the Crown Court on the basis that the plea was equivocal and if the Crown Court decides that the plea was equivocal, it will remit the case to the magistrates to rehear on a not guilty plea.

9. Idris (aged 15) is found guilty in the Youth Court of committing a burglary involving the theft of £25,000 worth of jewellery. He is now due to be sentenced for the crime. Which of the following propositions is correct?

The Youth Court:

[A] May commit him for sentence to the Crown Court.
[B] Must deal with him itself.
[C] Must commit him for sentence to the Crown Court.
[D] May commit him for sentence to the adult Magistrates' Court.

10. Francesca (aged 22) is convicted of theft by the Greenbridge Magistrates' Court. Being of the opinion that the offence is so serious that greater punishment should be inflicted for the offence than they have power to impose, the Greenbridge magistrates commit her for sentence under the Magistrates' Courts Act 1980, s. 38, to the Pencaster Crown Court. The Pencaster Crown Court imposes a sentence of 3 months' imprisonment. Francesca now wishes to appeal to the Court of Appeal against sentence.

Which one of the following statements is correct?

[A] Francesca may appeal as of right.
[B] Francesca may appeal with leave of the single judge of the Court of Appeal.
[C] Francesca may appeal with leave of the sentencing judge.
[D] Francesca cannot appeal to the Court of Appeal.

11. Nicky is aged 14. He appears in the Youth Court, charged alone with several burglaries of dwelling houses (such burglary being punishable with up to 14 years' imprisonment following conviction on indictment in the case of an adult offender). The value of property stolen in the burglaries is over £20,000. The Youth Court decides to hold proceedings with a view to committing Nicky to the Crown Court for trial.

Assuming there is a prima facie case against Nicky, which one of the following statements is correct?

[A] He can be committed for trial because a Crown Court judge might lawfully pass a sentence under s. 53(2) of the Children and Young Persons Act 1933.
[B] He must be committed for trial because the Youth Court has no jurisdiction to try a case where the offence carries a sentence of 14 years' imprisonment or more.
[C] He cannot be committed for trial because he is not charged together with an adult and a sentence under s. 53(2) of the Children and Young Persons Act 1933 would not be lawful in his case.
[D] He cannot be committed for trial because juveniles cannot be tried in the Crown Court for burglary of a dwelling.

12. James fails to attend his summary trial for an offence of theft by shoplifting. At his last appearance before the court on that charge, he was told of the time and date of his trial. The magistrates:

[A] Must adjourn the case until James is present.
[B] Have a discretion to hear the case on the basis of a not guilty plea.
[C] Must proceed to hear the case on the basis of a not guilty plea.
[D] Must proceed to deal with the case and, as James has failed to appear, have a discretion as to whether to treat him as if he had pleaded guilty.

13. Jacob is arrested in connection with an offence of robbery. On Jacob's arrival at the Police Station, a decision to detain him is made at 8 am by Police Constable Brown, who is not involved in the investigation. Reviews of detention are held by Sergeant Green at 2 pm and 11 pm. Jacob is given substantial meals at 12.30 pm and 6 pm and short breaks in the interrogation every two hours. He has now been in custody for 23 hours without charge, and consults a solicitor. What advice should his solicitor give him about his detention?

[A] The detention should have been reviewed at 2 pm, 8 pm and 2 am.
[B] The detention should have been reviewed at 2 pm, 8 pm and 2 am, and those reviews and their original decision to detain should have been carried out by officers of higher ranks.
[C] The times of the reviews are correct but those reviews, and the original decision to detain, should have been carried out by officers of higher ranks.
[D] He has no legitimate ground of complaint.

14. Kevin is convicted in the Magistrates' Court of burglary. He now wishes to apply for judicial review of his conviction. In order to do so, he must *first*:

[A] Serve notice on the Magistrates' Court and on the High Court of his intention to apply for judicial review.
[B] Apply to the High Court for leave to make the application for judicial review.
[C] Serve his application for judicial review on the Magistrates' Court, the High Court and the prosecution.
[D] Issue a summons against the prosecution to appear in the High Court.

15. Harry elects summary trial on a charge of assault occasioning actual bodily harm. He is found guilty and fined. He wishes to appeal against conviction, but not against sentence. He asks you for advice as to any adverse implications for him. You should advise him that the Crown Court:

[A] Can order him to pay the prosecution's costs but cannot increase the sentence.
[B] Cannot order him to pay the prosecution's costs but can increase his sentence to the maximum which the magistrates could have imposed.
[C] Can order him to pay the prosecution's costs and can increase the sentence to the maximum which the magistrates could have imposed.
[D] Can order him to pay the prosecution's costs and can increase the sentence to the maximum which the Crown Court could have imposed if he had been tried on indictment.

16. Robbie, aged 20, pleads guilty at the Yellowbrick Crown Court to a charge of robbery. You mitigate on his behalf and draw to the court's attention the 'exceptional circumstances' disclosed in his pre-sentence report, namely that he lives with his disabled mother who is considerably reliant upon him. Which one of the following sentences will the court NOT be able to impose:

[A] A sentence of 2 years' imprisonment suspended for 2 years.
[B] A sentence of 2 years' detention in a young offender institution.
[C] A combination order.
[D] A community service order.

17. Martha is charged on indictment with murder. Before arraignment her counsel raises the issue of her fitness to plead. The judge decides that she is unfit to plead and makes a hospital order in respect of her. This procedure is flawed in that:

[A] The issue of fitness to plead should only be raised at the end of the prosecution's case.
[B] The issue of fitness to plead should have been determined by a jury.
[C] A hospital order is not an appropriate response to a finding of unfitness to plead.
[D] The issue of fitness to plead cannot be raised when the charge is murder.

18. Members of a jury are unable to reach a verdict and the judge discharges them. Which one of the following statements is correct?

[A] There must be a re-trial.
[B] There may be a re-trial if the prosecution wish to proceed.
[C] The charge against the defendant is left on the file marked not to be proceeded with unless the Crown Court or the Court of Appeal gives leave.
[D] The defendant is acquitted.

19. Nickie, aged 19, appears at the Picklewig Crown Court on committal for sentence from the Picklegown Magistrates' Court on 2 charges of theft from her employer. The judge imposes a sentence of 9 months' detention in a young offender institution in respect of the first charge and a probation order for 12 months in respect of the second. The judge:

[A] Has power to impose these 2 sentences on the same occasion.
[B] Has no power to impose these 2 sentences on the same occasion but it would be unprofessional for counsel to correct the judge in respect of the mistake.
[C] Has power to impose these 2 sentences on the same occasion subject to Nickie's consent.
[D] Has no power to impose the 2 sentences on the same occasion and it would be the professional duty of counsel to draw the judge's attention to the mistake.

20. Sheila was committed for trial on a charge of theft of a camera, this being the only charge before the magistrates. The papers before the magistrates when they decided to commit the case for trial disclosed, among other things, that she was arrested the day after the alleged theft when she tried to sell the camera, for a fraction of its usual price, to a plain clothes policeman. The indictment contains a single count alleging theft. At the end of the prosecution's evidence in the Crown Court, the prosecution seek to add a second count alleging handling stolen goods, namely the camera. This application:

[A] Will succeed, unless, having regard to the merits of the case and the possibility of adjourning, the new count cannot be added without injustice to Sheila.
[B] Will fail, because the counts in the indictment must correspond with the charges found by the magistrates on committal for trial.
[C] Will fail, because all applications relating to the form of the indictment must be made on arraignment, and it is now too late.
[D] Is unnecessary because the prosecution have an absolute right to amend the form of an indictment at any time.

21. Darren pleads guilty in the Magistrates' Court to theft. He now tells you that the offence was in fact committed by Eric, who bullied him into taking the blame for it, saying that Darren's little boy 'would live to regret it' if he did not. Darren now wishes to appeal to the Crown Court. In this situation:

[A] He has no right to appeal against conviction, but may do so with the leave of the Crown Court, and, if leave is given, the case will be reheard in the Crown Court.
[B] He has no right to appeal against conviction but may challenge the validity of the plea, and, if that challenge is successful, the case will be remitted to the magistrates for rehearing.
[C] He has no right to appeal against conviction, but may do so with the leave of the Magistrates' Court, and if leave is given, the case will be reheard in the Crown Court.
[D] He has the right to appeal against conviction by serving notice on the Magistrates' Court and the magistrates will rehear the case themselves.

22. An indictment contains a single count for robbery. The judge in her summing up directs the jury that they may find the defendant 'not guilty of robbery but guilty of theft', and the jury bring in such a verdict. Their verdict is:

[A] Valid, because robbery includes by implication an allegation of an offence of theft.
[B] Valid, because theft is a less serious offence than robbery.
[C] Invalid, because sufficient particulars for a count alleging theft cannot be arrived at by deleting particulars from the existing robbery count.
[D] Invalid, because the jury is only empowered to return a verdict in respect of those offences for which the accused has been arraigned.

23. Toby is charged with handling stolen goods. Just before arraignment he tells you that he would plead guilty if he could be sure that he would not receive a custodial sentence. You ask to see the judge in his chambers. Which one of the following statements is INCORRECT?

[A] Counsel for the defence may discuss the case with the judge in chambers provided that prosecuting counsel and a shorthand writer are present as well.
[B] Counsel may discuss the case with the judge but only in open court.
[C] The judge may indicate that the sentence will or will not take a particular form (e.g., custody) irrespective of whether the defendant pleads guilty or is found guilty.
[D] If the judge indicates that a sentence will or will not take a particular form, the judge must subsequently pass a sentence that is consistent with that indication.

24. Rupert, aged 16, appears in the Toughbench Youth Court and pleads guilty to 4 charges of indecent assault on women. The offences are triable either way and the maximum sentence for each offence is 10 years. Which one of the following statements about the magistrates' powers is correct?

When sentencing, the magistrates may:

[A] Impose a maximum custodial sentence of 12 months in aggregate for the offences.
[B] Impose a maximum custodial sentence of 6 months in aggregate for the offences.
[C] Commit him to the Crown Court for sentence where he may be sentenced to a maximum custodial sentence of 12 months per offence to run consecutively, amounting to 4 years in aggregate.
[D] Commit him to the Crown Court for sentence where he may be sentenced to a maximum custodial sentence of 10 years per offence to run concurrently, amounting to 10 years in aggregate.

25. At the end of the prosecution case, counsel for the defence makes a submission of no case to answer. The judge rejects this submission and orders the trial to continue. The alleged defect in the prosecution case is rectified by cross-examination of the defence witnesses. The defendant is convicted, and appeals solely on the basis that the judge was wrong to reject the submission.

Assuming that the judge was wrong in law to reject the submission, which of the following actions is the Court of Appeal most likely to take?

[A] Quash the conviction, because, had the judge not erred, the defendant would have been acquitted.
[B] Quash the conviction, and order a *venire de novo*.
[C] Uphold the conviction if satisfied that the judge directed the jury properly when he summed up.
[D] Examine the evidence given during both the prosecution and defence cases, and decide the appeal on that basis.

26. John is charged with indecent assault upon Tracey. It is alleged that the assault took place in one of the cubicles at the physiotherapy department of the hospital where John works as a porter. The only prosecution evidence is that of Tracey and her mother (who says that Tracey returned home in a distressed state on the day in question). After the jury have retired, they send a note to the judge asking for further evidence, namely whether or not the adjacent cubicles were in use at the time of the alleged assault so that any protests by Tracey might have been heard. As counsel in the case, you are asked by the judge whether he can comply with this request. What should you say to him?

[A] The jury are only entitled to hear additional evidence if the judge first gives leave to the prosecution to re-open their case.
[B] The jury are entitled to ask for any additional evidence provided that the evidence is given in open court, in the presence of the accused and of both counsel.
[C] The jury are not entitled to ask any questions once they have retired.
[D] The jury are not entitled to hear additional evidence after they have retired.

27. Stan has been remanded in custody by Exchester Magistrates' Court following a fully argued bail application. He wishes to challenge the refusal of bail. Which one of the following statements is correct?

[A] If Stan applies to the Crown Court and the judge refuses bail, Stan can only apply to the High Court with leave of the Crown Court judge or of a High Court judge.
[B] If Stan applies to the High Court and the judge refuses bail, Stan cannot then apply to the Crown Court.
[C] Stan may apply to either the High Court or the Crown Court and then, if unsuccessful, to the other one but should inform the second court of the unsuccessful application.
[D] The High Court only has jurisdiction if the grounds for obtaining a writ of habeas corpus are satisfied.

28. Bill, aged 18, appears at the Carhot Magistrates' Court and is convicted of aggravated motor vehicle taking which was alleged to have occurred in Carhot Green. He has 3 previous findings of guilt for taking motor vehicles without consent for which he received an Attendance Centre Order, a Supervision Order and a Community Service Order respectively. The offence is very prevalent in the Carhot area. When sentencing, the Carhot magistrates should NOT have regard to one of the following considerations. Which one?

[A] The need to impose an 'exemplary' sentence to serve as an example to other young offenders.
[B] The prevalence of the offence in that area.
[C] The offender's previous offences and any failure to respond to previous sentences.
[D] The need to impose a sentence which is commensurate with the seriousness of the offence.

29. Daniel is charged with burglary contrary to s. 9(1)(b) of the Theft Act 1968 at Pencaster Crown Court, in that he entered a building as a trespasser and stole a television set. The evidence, from both the prosecution and the defence, shows that he had had permission both to enter the building and to borrow the television set, but that he had failed to return it when he should because he had decided to keep it permanently. Daniel is convicted and now appeals to the Court of Appeal. The Court of Appeal accepts that he did not enter as a trespasser, and that he had permission to borrow the television set, but holds that he had wrongfully and dishonestly retained it and did not intend to return it to its owner. In these circumstances, which of the following courses of action is the Court of Appeal most likely to adopt?

[A] It will quash the conviction.
[B] It will uphold the conviction.
[C] It will quash the conviction, but substitute a conviction for theft.
[D] It will quash the conviction and order a re-trial.

30. Albert is convicted of a series of thefts and related offences (some summary and some triable either way) at the Newtown Magistrates' Court. The magistrates now consider that the combination of offences is so serious that greater punishment should be inflicted than they have power to impose. In these circumstances the magistrates:

[A] Have no choice but to sentence him themselves.
[B] May commit the triable either way offences to the Crown Court for sentence, but may not commit the summary offences.
[C] May commit the triable either way offences to the Crown Court for sentence, but must adjourn the summary offences *sine die*.
[D] May commit all the offences to the Crown Court for sentence.

31. If a jury which has been given a majority verdict direction is still unable to reach a verdict, the judge may give them further directions. According to the decisions of the Court of Appeal these further directions must NOT include one of the following elements. Which one?

[A] That the jurors have a duty to act not only as individuals but also collectively.
[B] That jurors should be willing to give and take.
[C] That jurors should be prepared to alter their views if they can do so and still remain consistent to the oath which they have taken.
[D] That jurors should bear in mind the inconvenience of a fresh trial if they cannot reach a verdict.

32. Alan was committed to the Crown Court for trial on a charge of blackmail. The papers before the magistrates when they took the decision to commit also indicated that Alan had perpetrated an offence of theft (which was wholly unconnected with the alleged blackmail); however Alan was not committed on any charge of theft. The prosecution preferred two indictments – one containing the count of blackmail, the other a count of theft. At the trial of the blackmail indictment Alan was acquitted. At the trial of the theft indictment an application by Alan's counsel to have the indictment quashed was rejected by the trial judge.

The trial judge's decision was:

[A] Incorrect because the prosecution can never prefer an indictment which charges an offence on which there was no committal for trial.
[B] Incorrect because the prosecution can only prefer an indictment which charges an offence on which there was no committal if the offence in question could properly be joined (in the same indictment) with the offence(s) on which there was a committal.
[C] Correct because the prosecution can always prefer an indictment in respect of any offence which is disclosed by the committal papers (whether or not there has been a committal on that charge).
[D] Correct because the prosecution can prefer an indictment in respect of any offence which falls within the same Statute as an offence for which an accused has been committed.

33. On 16 April 1996 Peter was placed on probation for two years by Grimchester Crown Court for an offence of theft. In July 1998 he appears before the Doomchester Crown Court and pleads guilty to an offence of obtaining property by deception, this offence having been committed on 1 April 1998. The following statements relate to the powers of Doomchester Crown Court to deal with the offence of theft from 1996. Only one of these statements is correct. Which one?

[A] No action can be taken in respect of the theft as the date of the conviction for the later offence is more than 2 years after the date on which the probation order was made.
[B] Doomchester Crown Court can re-sentence in respect of the theft but only with the consent of Grimchester Crown Court.
[C] Doomchester Crown Court can re-sentence in respect of the theft but can only pass a non-custodial sentence for the theft.
[D] Doomchester Crown Court can re-sentence in respect of the theft and can pass a custodial or non-custodial sentence for the theft.

34. Where the Court of Appeal considers the making of an order for loss of time spent in custody pending an appeal, and assuming that the Court adopts the approach set out in the 1980 *Practice Direction* on loss of time, which one of the following statements is correct?

[A] The order is unlikely to be made when leave to appeal is refused by the single judge of the Court of Appeal, if grounds of appeal are settled by counsel and supported by his written opinion.
[B] The order is unlikely to be made where leave to appeal is refused by the full Court of Appeal, if grounds of appeal are settled by counsel and supported by his written opinion.
[C] Both [A] and [B] are correct.
[D] Neither [A] nor [B] is correct.

35. Arnold, aged 20, is sentenced to 2 years' imprisonment by a Crown Court judge. He wishes to appeal against this sentence. In these circumstances, which one of the following statements is correct?

[A] Arnold does not need leave to appeal, because the sentence is wrong in law.
[B] Arnold can only get leave from the single judge of the Court of Appeal, because the appeal is against sentence.
[C] Arnold can appeal only if he obtains the leave of the trial judge.
[D] Arnold may either get leave to appeal from the single judge of the Court of Appeal, or a certificate from the trial judge that the case is fit for appeal.

CRIMINAL EVIDENCE

36. Gareth, a Welsh nationalist, is charged with the murder of Harry, an English motorist. The prosecution case is that Gareth, while standing on a bridge over a busy road, rolled a granite boulder over the edge and onto the road; and that the boulder fell through the windscreen of Harry's car, causing him multiple injuries from which he died within minutes. Gareth gives evidence admitting these facts but denying that he intended to cause death or serious bodily harm to Harry. Which of the following would be the best way in which to direct the jury on the question whether they may infer that Gareth intended death or serious bodily harm as a result of his actions?

[A] 'You should decide whether Gareth intended death or serious bodily harm by reference to all the evidence, drawing such inferences as appear proper in the circumstances.'
[B] 'You are not entitled to infer that Gareth intended death or serious bodily harm as a result of his actions.'
[C] 'If you are satisfied that death or serious bodily harm was a natural and probable consequence of Gareth's actions, then you should infer that he intended death or serious bodily harm as a result of those actions.'
[D] 'You may only infer that Gareth intended death or serious bodily harm as a result of his actions if he has failed to satisfy you that he did not intend death or serious bodily harm.'

37. Jane is charged on indictment with obtaining property by deception from Harrods, having ordered goods on a credit account using a false name. At the trial, counsel for Jane, on her behalf, admits that she had opened this account. May the prosecution rely on counsel's admission?

[A] No, because the admission was not in writing.
[B] Yes, because the admission was made orally in court.
[C] No, because counsel's admission can never bind Jane.
[D] Yes, because although the admission is inadmissible, the judge will exercise his discretion to admit it.

38. Fred and Harry are jointly charged with blackmailing their employer. Fred pleads not guilty; Harry pleads guilty. The prosecution wish to call Fred's wife, Ghisha, and Harry's wife, Irene, to give evidence. Are Ghisha and Irene competent and compellable to give evidence for the prosecution?

[A] Ghisha is competent and compellable; Irene is competent but not compellable.
[B] Ghisha is competent but not compellable; Irene is competent and compellable.
[C] Both Ghisha and Irene are competent but not compellable.
[D] Both Ghisha and Irene are competent and compellable.

39. At a trial on indictment, the jury, after an hour's retirement to consider their verdict, return to the court. The foreman tells the judge that a number of the jurors have expressed difficulty in deciding whether the prosecution have discharged the burden of proof because they do not understand the meaning of proof 'beyond reasonable doubt'. Which of the following would be the best way for the judge to respond?

[A] 'I cannot help you, because if I attempted any gloss upon the words, or were to give you an analogy, it might be misleading.'
[B] 'It means exactly what it says: a doubt for which one could give reasons if asked.'
[C] 'It means the sort of doubt which might affect you in the conduct of your everyday affairs.'
[D] 'It means the kind of doubt which, when you are dealing with matters of importance in your own affairs, you allow to influence you one way or the other.'

40. Michael is charged with indecently assaulting Nora. The case for the prosecution is that he and Nora were sitting together in a train travelling from London to Oxford and that shortly after the train passed through Reading, Michael put out his hand and touched Nora's breasts. Michael admits that he and Nora were sitting together in the train, but denies that he touched her. When the police (lawfully) searched Michael's briefcase they discovered a number of pornographic magazines containing pictures of naked women. Will evidence of this discovery be admitted at Michael's trial?

[A] Yes, because it is evidence of Michael's lustful disposition.
[B] Yes, because it rebuts Michael's denial of the offence.
[C] No, because any probative value it may have is outweighed by its prejudicial effect.
[D] No, because although highly relevant, it should be excluded under s. 78 of the Police and Criminal Evidence Act 1984.

41. Carlos is charged with murder and raises the defence of diminished responsibility. Which party bears the evidential and legal burdens in relation to the defence raised; and what standard of proof is required to discharge the legal burden on that defence?

[A] The evidential burden is on the defence; the legal burden is on the prosecution and will be discharged by proof beyond reasonable doubt.
[B] The evidential burden is on the defence; the legal burden is also on the defence and will be discharged by raising a reasonable doubt.
[C] The evidential burden is on the defence; the legal burden is also on the defence and will be discharged by proof on a balance of probabilities.
[D] The evidential burden is on the prosecution; the legal burden is on the defence and will be discharged by proof beyond reasonable doubt.

42. Patrick, who is French, is charged with the theft of a packet of batteries from a shop in High Holborn. It is alleged that he entered the shop, took the batteries from a shelf, put them into his pocket, rushed out of the shop, and ran away. At his trial (in London), he gives evidence through an interpreter. Cross-examined about his knowledge of English, he denies that he can speak English. The prosecution now wish to introduce evidence to show that Patrick is fluent in English. Should they be allowed to do so?

[A] Yes, because the jury is entitled to know that Patrick was prepared to lie on oath.
[B] Yes, because such evidence is likely to lead the jury to reappraise Patrick's evidence on the facts in issue in the case.
[C] No, because of the rule of finality of answers to questions concerning collateral matters.
[D] There is no clear answer, because the cases show that the difference between questions going to credit and questions going to the issue has been reduced to vanishing point.

43. Tom, who has previous convictions for offences of dishonesty, is charged with burglary. He does not give evidence but his counsel puts to the chief witness for the prosecution that he (the witness) has 2 previous convictions for theft, as in fact is the case. The witness denies that he has such convictions. On these facts, consider the following propositions.

(i) Counsel for the prosecution may make a formal admission that the witness has the 2 convictions for theft.
(ii) Counsel for the defence may prove the fact of the convictions for theft.
(iii) Tom has put his character in issue and the prosecution, with the leave of the judge, may call evidence of Tom's previous convictions.

Which of these propositions is INCORRECT?

[A] (i) only.
[B] (i) and (ii), but not (iii).
[C] (ii) and (iii), but not (i).
[D] (iii) only.

44. Lawrence is charged with murder, and relies on the defence of self-defence. Shortly after the incident, he told Malcolm, a friend, that his defence would be one of self-defence. At the trial, Lawrence gives evidence of self-defence. Consider the following 2 statements:

(i) Lawrence's words to Malcolm are prima facie inadmissible as a previous consistent statement.
(ii) Lawrence's words to Malcolm are admissible if the prosecution put it to Lawrence that he has invented the defence only after hearing the prosecution case to serve his own purposes at the trial.

Which of the above statements is correct?

[A] Only (i).
[B] Only (ii).
[C] Neither.
[D] Both.

45. Which of the following statements best describes the position at trial where a witness has previously identified the accused out of court?

[A] Evidence of the out-of-court identification is inadmissible.
[B] Evidence of the out-of-court identification is admissible, but only after the witness has identified the accused in court.
[C] Evidence of the out-of-court identification is admissible, but only if the witness has been unable to identify the accused in court.
[D] Evidence of the out-of-court identification is admissible and this should be elicited prior to the witness identifying the accused in court.

46. Alf is charged with the murder of a woman cyclist by deliberately driving his car at her. The prosecution can prove that in the week before the alleged murder, in separate incidents Alf had knocked 2 other women cyclists off their bicycles. Alf's defence is accident. Is the evidence of the other incidents admissible:

[A] No, because its prejudicial effect outweighs its probative value.
[B] No, because it is irrelevant.
[C] Yes, because its probative value outweighs its prejudicial effect.
[D] Yes, because similar fact evidence is always admissible to rebut a defence of accident.

47. Gregory and Julia are jointly charged with obtaining property by deception from Ian, Julia's ex-husband. They both plead not guilty. The prosecution wish to call Harriet, Gregory's wife. Julia wishes to call Kenneth, her husband, to give evidence on her behalf. Are Harriet and Kenneth competent and compellable?

[A] Harriet is competent but not compellable for the prosecution; Kenneth is competent but not compellable on behalf of Julia.
[B] Harriet is competent and compellable for the prosecution; Kenneth is competent and compellable on behalf of Julia.
[C] Harriet is competent but not compellable for the prosecution; Kenneth is competent and compellable on behalf of Julia.
[D] Harriet is competent and compellable for the prosecution; Kenneth is competent but not compellable on behalf of Julia.

48. John and his wife Michelle have been living apart for the past 2 years. Michelle decided to refuse John any further access to the 2 children aged 8 and 10, as the children told her that their father was drunk and violent on the last 2 visits. On being refused access, John turned up at Michelle's house where he assaulted her and the children. In subsequent criminal proceedings the prosecution intend to call Michelle as the main prosecution witness. She is reluctant to testify as she is frightened of John. Is Michelle competent *and* compellable for the prosecution?

[A] Yes, because Michelle is separated from John.
[B] Yes, because of the nature of the offences concerned.
[C] No, because although competent Michelle is not compellable.
[D] No, because they are still married and she is neither competent nor compellable.

49. Morgan is charged with indecently assaulting a 9-year-old girl in the town park at 4 pm on 11 September last year. His defence is mistaken identity. He told the police officer investigating the incident that he left work early that day in order to accompany his wife to the health clinic but did not get home until after she had left because he missed the bus. At trial, he testifies that, after he had missed the bus, he took a short cut through the town park that afternoon; and that he omitted to state this to the officer because he had been in trouble with the police before and he was afraid that 'they would try to pin things on him again'. The judge allows the prosecution to cross-examine Morgan on his previous conviction for indecent exposure. *On the facts given,* the best justification for this ruling is that:

[A] He is not a credible witness.
[B] He has cast imputations on the character of a prosecution witness.
[C] He has already revealed his character to the jury.
[D] The previous conviction shows a general propensity towards offences of a sexual nature.

50. The following statements concern evidence of the character of the accused. Only one is correct. Which one?

[A] At common law, the only exception to the general rule that the prosecution is not entitled to adduce evidence of the accused's bad character is where the accused has adduced evidence of his good character.
[B] Where an accused elects not to testify but relies on wholly exculpatory statements made to the police, and evidence of the good character of the accused is properly admitted in evidence, the judge should direct the jury on the relevance of this evidence in relation to the guilt of the accused.
[C] The word 'character' as used in proviso (f) to s. 1 of the Criminal Evidence Act 1898 refers only to general reputation.
[D] An accused who elects to testify may not be asked any question if it would tend directly to incriminate him as to the offence charged.

51. David is a porter at a large office block. He is required to keep a detailed log of all visitors, and any incidents that may occur. One day, Francis visited the block, asking to see George, who works in the block. George met Francis in the entrance hall. A fight broke out and George was injured. Shortly afterwards, David made an entry in his log-book recording the incident. Francis has now been charged with causing George grievous bodily harm. By the date of the trial, David has no recollection of the incident at all. Is the entry in David's log-book admissible?

[A] No, because hearsay.
[B] Yes, in principle, under the Criminal Justice Act 1988, s. 24.
[C] Yes, in principle, under the Criminal Justice Act 1988, s. 23.
[D] Yes, as original evidence.

52. Amanda is charged with blackmail. Police officers claim that when they called at Amanda's house on a totally unrelated matter (routine door-to-door enquiries about a missing child), Amanda, on seeing them, had said: 'It's about the blackmail isn't it? I'm sorry. I knew you'd catch me sooner or later.' Amanda admits that the officers called and asked about a missing child, but categorically denies that she ever made the alleged confession: she alleges that the officers have invented the confession (but does not allege any other improper behaviour on their part). The prosecution intend to call the police officers to prove Amanda's confession. Is such evidence admissible?

[A] Yes, but only if the judge holds a voir dire and gives a ruling to this effect.
[B] No, because Amanda categorically denies making the confession.
[C] Yes, and without recourse to a voir dire.
[D] No, because hearsay.

53. Sam is charged with murdering his wife, Tina, by stabbing her with a knife. The prosecution case is that the reason for the offence was the discovery by Sam that Tina was having an adulterous affair with his best friend, Victor. According to Sam, however, he made no such discovery. The day before the alleged murder, Tina wrote a letter to Vera, a friend, stating: 'Yesterday, Sam discovered me and Victor in bed together!' Are the contents of this letter admissible?

[A] No, because hearsay.
[B] Yes, under the Criminal Justice Act 1988, s. 24, subject to the discretion to exclude under s. 25.
[C] Yes, as a dying declaration.
[D] Yes, under the Criminal Justice Act 1988, s. 23, subject to the discretion to exclude under s. 25.

54. Plain clothes police officers, without announcing that they were police officers, entered 'Eric's Minimarket' and bought some whisky. As a result of this purchase, Eric was subsequently charged with selling liquor without a licence. At the trial, counsel for Eric submits that evidence of the purchase should be excluded under the Police and Criminal Evidence Act 1984, s. 78. What should the court do?

[A] Admit the evidence, because to do so has no adverse effect on the fairness of the proceedings.
[B] Admit the evidence, because the circumstances in which it was obtained are irrelevant.
[C] Exclude the evidence, because of the officers' trickery.
[D] Exclude the evidence, because before purchasing the whisky, the officers should have administered a caution.

55. Anthony is charged with theft. Shortly after his arrest he made a full confession to the charge. At the trial evidence is given by his girlfriend, Beatrice, that she had seen him during his detention for questioning and had told him that if he confessed he would get bail. His counsel submits that the confession should be excluded under the Police and Criminal Evidence Act 1984, s. 76(2)(b) (likelihood of unreliability). The trial judge finds that Beatrice probably did make the statement about bail but nevertheless rules that the confession is admissible. This ruling could have been correct on only one of the following grounds. Which one?

[A] Under s. 76, a confession is always admissible if obtained by someone other than a person in authority.
[B] The judge was satisfied that Anthony's confession was true.
[C] The judge was satisfied that Anthony's confession was not obtained in consequence of Beatrice's statement.
[D] There is an overriding discretion to ignore the effect of s. 76(2)(b) and include confession statements.

56. Michael, aged 20, is tried on indictment for indecent assault. The prosecution case depends substantially on a confession he made to 2 police officers who interviewed him after his arrest. No other person was present at the interview. The trial judge on a voir dire relating to the admissibility of this confession concludes that Michael is 'mentally handicapped' (as defined in the Police and Criminal Evidence Act 1984). Which of the following statements about this case is correct?

[A] The judge, having concluded that Michael is mentally handicapped, is required by law to exclude Michael's confession.
[B] If the judge admits Michael's confession, she is required by law to warn the jury that there is a special need for caution before convicting the accused in reliance on the confession.
[C] Having regard to his mental handicap, Michael is eligible to give unsworn evidence.
[D] Michael is eligible to give sworn evidence but only if he satisfies the judge that he understands the divine sanction of the oath.

57. Peter and Rupert were charged with an armed bank robbery. Photographs which had been taken by a security camera automatically at 5-second intervals during the course of the raid, were produced at the trial. No identification witnesses were called, but the jury were invited to look at the photographs, look at the defendants in the dock and conclude, if they thought it right to do so, that the men in the photographs were in fact the men in the dock. Peter and Rupert were convicted, and appeal on the ground that the photographs were improperly admitted. Is the appeal likely to succeed?

[A] Yes, because admission of the photographs was in breach of the hearsay rule.
[B] No, because the photographs were admissible under the Criminal Justice Act 1988, s. 24.
[C] Yes, because the admission of the photographs was in breach of the rule against previous consistent statements.
[D] No, because photographs are in a class of their own to which neither the rule against hearsay nor the rule against previous consistent statements applies.

58. Rob is charged with murdering Susan. Tom, an associate of Rob, signs a death-bed statement to the effect that he, not Rob, murdered Susan. Tom dies before Rob's trial. Subject to any discretion that the judge may have to exclude it, Tom's statement is admissible. On what basis?

[A] Under the Police and Criminal Evidence Act 1984, s. 76 as a confession.
[B] Under the Criminal Justice Act 1988, s. 23.
[C] As part of the *res gestae*.
[D] As a dying declaration.

59. Robin is charged with handling a stolen video recorder. His defence is that he purchased it, without knowledge or belief that it was stolen, from a former neighbour who has since emigrated. He claims that the neighbour had said to him at the time of the purchase 'I bought it from a shop last Christmas, though I haven't kept the receipt or guarantee.' At trial, evidence of what the neighbour allegedly said to him will be admissible, for the defence. On what basis?

[A] As part of the *res gestae*.
[B] As evidence of Robin's lack of knowledge or belief that the goods were stolen.
[C] As evidence that the goods were not stolen.
[D] Under s. 23 of the Criminal Justice Act 1988.

60. Whenever a trial judge directs the jury on the proper use of lies by the accused to support evidence of guilt, the direction should make it clear to the jury that they should be satisfied on all the following matters except one. Which one?

[A] That the lie was deliberate.
[B] That the lie was in writing or otherwise recorded in documentary form.
[C] That there was no innocent motive for the lie.
[D] That the lie relates to a material issue.

61. Joan is charged with theft. At her trial she challenges under the Police and Criminal Evidence Act 1984, s. 76(2)(b) (likelihood of unreliability) the admissibility of a confession she made to the police. The judge rules that the confession is admissible holding that (1) s. 76(2)(b) requires some element of improper conduct on the part of the interrogator (which is absent in Joan's case); and (2) the test is whether the confession Joan actually made was obtained in consequence of anything said or done which was likely, in the circumstances existing at the time, to render unreliable 'any confession which might be made by her in consequence thereof'. Is the judge's ruling on these points correct or incorrect?

[A] Correct on the first point, incorrect on the second.
[B] Correct on both points.
[C] Incorrect on the first point, correct on the second.
[D] Incorrect on both points.

62. John is suspected of committing a series of burglaries. The police arrested him and detained him for questioning. He made a full confession and was charged with the burglaries. At his trial, he challenges the admissibility of the confession, representing that it was obtained by oppression. The trial judge makes two rulings: (1) that she will only hold a voir dire if the defence adduce some evidence in support of their representation; and (2) that if such a voir dire does take place, she will be entitled to enquire into the truth or falsity of the confession. Is the judge's ruling on these points correct or incorrect?

[A] Incorrect on both points.
[B] Correct on both points.
[C] Incorrect on the first point, correct on the second.
[D] Correct on the first point, incorrect on the second.

63. Jim was overtaken by a yellow Ford Escort car and made a mental note of the registration number, XYZ 1. Moments later the Escort pulled out to overtake on the brow of a hill and an oncoming car driven by Ken was forced to swerve off the road and into a ditch. Jim stopped and told a police officer, Luke, what he had seen, including the registration number of the Ford Escort. Luke made a written note of Jim's statement (but this was not read back to Jim nor signed by Jim). The Ford Escort is traced to Adam who is charged with dangerous driving. Luke has since died. Is Luke's note admissible?

[A] No, because hearsay.
[B] Yes, in principle, under the Criminal Justice Act 1988, s. 23.
[C] Yes, in principle, under the Criminal Justice Act 1988, s. 24.
[D] Yes, as a declaration in the course of duty by a person deceased at the time of trial.

64. Same facts as in Question 63 above, except that Jim told Ken (the driver of the car which was forced into the ditch) what he had seen and Ken relayed Jim's statement to Luke who wrote it down. Is Luke's note admissible?

[A] No, because hearsay.
[B] Yes, under the Criminal Justice Act 1988, s. 23 (subject to the discretion to exclude under s. 25 and/or the requirement of leave under s. 26).
[C] Yes, under the Criminal Justice Act 1988, s. 24 (subject to the discretion to exclude under s. 25 and/or the requirement of leave under s. 26).
[D] Yes, under the public records exception.

65. Bill is charged with theft. The case against him depends substantially on the correctness of a visual identification of him by Clare, which Bill alleges to be mistaken. At the trial, the judge comes to the conclusion that the quality of Clare's identification evidence is poor. What should he do?

[A] Direct an acquittal, whatever the nature of the other evidence in the case.
[B] Direct an acquittal, unless there is other evidence, which must be corroboration in the strict sense, which goes to support the correctness of the identification evidence.
[C] Direct an acquittal, unless there is other evidence, whether or not corroboration in the strict sense, which goes to support the correctness of the identification evidence.
[D] As in [C], but subject to the proviso that if there is supportive evidence, he must direct the jury that if he had thought there was insufficient identification evidence, he would have directed them to acquit.

66. Victor and Walter are charged with handling stolen goods, namely machine tools which, the prosecution allege, were stolen from XYZ (Machine Tools) Ltd. On being questioned by the police, Victor and Walter admit that the goods must have originally come from XYZ (Machine Tools) Ltd, because they saw the labels attached to the boxes in which they were originally packed, which read: 'XYZ (Machine Tools) Ltd. Do not remove.' However, they also say that they bought the tools from a man they had arranged to meet in a pub, having seen an advert in the local paper that tools were for sale and having rung the number given. At the trial, the prosecution seek to establish that the goods were stolen from XYZ (Machine Tools) Ltd by relying on the admissions made by Victor and Walter as to their origin. Are these admissions admissible?

[A] No, because they were based solely on the reading of the labels and have no more evidential value than the labels themselves.
[B] Yes, not being hearsay, because the court is not concerned with the truth of the statements but with whether the statements were made.
[C] Yes, as admissions which, in the circumstances, are at least prima facie evidence that the goods were stolen.
[D] Yes in law, but open to exclusion under s. 78 of the Police and Criminal Evidence Act 1984.

67. Adam is standing trial for the murder of his wife. He will introduce evidence in support of his defence of provocation. At the trial the prosecution call a police officer who gives evidence that Adam, on being charged with the offence (and having been properly cautioned) remained completely silent. The defence accept that at that stage Adam failed to mention the facts he will rely on in support of his defence and also that they are facts which, in the circumstances existing at the time, Adam could reasonably have been expected to mention.

In these circumstances, consider the following statements:

(i) The court, in deciding whether there is a case to answer, may draw such inferences from Adam's failure (to mention the facts) as appear proper.
(ii) The court or jury, in deciding whether Adam is guilty of the offence charged, may draw such inferences from Adam's failure (to mention the facts) as appear proper.
(iii) Adam cannot be convicted of murder solely on an inference drawn from his failure (to mention the facts).

Which of these statements, if any, is accurate?

[A] None of them.
[B] (i) and (ii), but not (iii).
[C] (ii) and (iii), but not (i).
[D] All of them.

68. Michael is charged with assaulting Paul, a fellow employee. In his defence, Michael claims that he was acting in reasonable self defence (although Michael accepts that Paul had only lightly tapped him on the arm). Michael says in evidence that his mother died shortly before the alleged assault and he was feeling particularly sensitive at the time. He wishes to call a psychiatrist to give evidence that shortly after the alleged offence he, Michael, appeared to be a person suffering from severe sorrow following a recent bereavement; that he was likely to overreact to any adverse circumstances; but was not suffering from any mental illness. Will the psychiatrist's evidence be admissible?

[A] Yes, because it is the evidence of a qualified medical practitioner in his field of competence and is relevant to Michael's defence.
[B] Yes, but only in order to confirm the credibility of Michael's testimony as to his state of mind.
[C] No, because it is a self-serving statement in that the psychiatrist is simply repeating what Michael told him after the event.
[D] No, because the tribunal of fact does not need expert assistance in assessing Michael's alleged mental condition at the relevant time.

69. Marie was suspected by Naomi, a store detective, of shoplifting. She was detained and questioned about her suspected commission of the offence by Naomi and (according to Naomi) eventually admitted that she was shoplifting. At Marie's trial her counsel wishes to argue that her confession should be excluded under the Police and Criminal Evidence Act 1984, s. 78 because Naomi had interviewed Marie without complying with the Code of Practice for interviews made pursuant to s. 66 of that Act (Code C). Would such a course be justified?

[A] No, because Naomi's questioning of Marie could not have been an interview for the purposes of Code C.
[B] Yes, because on the facts the judge *could* conclude that Naomi was bound to comply with Code C.
[C] No, because only the police are bound to comply with Code C.
[D] Yes, because anyone who questions a suspect must comply with Code C.

70. George is charged with attempted burglary. At his trial a constable gives evidence that on his arrival at the scene of the crime, industrial premises surrounded by barbed-wire fencing, George was running away; that on arresting him he noticed that George's clothing was badly torn in several places; that he reasonably believed that the tears in George's clothing might have been the result of George's commission of the offence; that he told George of his belief and asked him to account for the condition of his clothing; and that George had replied: 'I don't have to, and I won't!'.

On these facts, may the court, in deciding whether there is a case to answer, draw such inferences as appear proper from George's refusal to account for the condition of his clothing?

[A] Yes.
[B] No, because such inferences can be drawn only from failure or refusal to account for the presence of objects on the person or in or on a person's clothing.
[C] No, because George was not told by the constable, when asking him to account for the condition of his clothing, the effect of failing or refusing to do so.
[D] No, because it is only in deciding whether George is guilty that the court may draw inferences from his refusal to account for the condition of his clothing.

APPENDIX 1

ANSWERS TO THE CIVIL MCT

CIVIL LITIGATION

1. C
2. D
3. B
4. C
5. D
6. B
7. D
8. B
9. A
10. D
11. B
12. A
13. A
14. D
15. C
16. C
17. D
18. A
19. D
20. C
21. B
22. D
23. B
24. A
25. B
26. D
27. D
28. C
29. A
30. C
31. D
32. D
33. B
34. B
35. B
36. C
37. A
38. A
39. C
40. A

CIVIL EVIDENCE

41. B
42. B
43. C
44. D
45. C
46. C
47. B
48. A
49. C
50. C
51. B
52. D
53. A
54. D
55. D
56. B
57. B
58. C
59. B
60. A
61. C
62. D
63. A
64. A
65. D
66. D
67. B
68. B
69. B
70. A

APPENDIX 2

ANSWERS TO THE CRIMINAL MCT

CRIMINAL LITIGATION AND SENTENCING

1. B	21. B		
2. C	22. A		
3. B	23. B		
4. C	24. A		
5. D	25. A		
6. D	26. D		
7. A	27. C		
8. D	28. A		
9. A	29. C		
10. D	30. D		
11. A	31. D		
12. B	32. B		
13. C	33. A		
14. B	34. A		
15. C	35. D		
16. A			
17. B			
18. B			
19. D			
20. A			

CRIMINAL EVIDENCE

36. A	51. B
37. B	52. C
38. B	53. D
39. D	54. A
40. C	55. C
41. C	56. B
42. C	57. D
43. D	58. B
44. D	59. B
45. D	60. B
46. C	61. C
47. C	62. A
48. B	63. C
49. C	64. A
50. B	65. C
	66. A
	67. D
	68. D
	69. B
	70. C

APPENDIX 3

NOTE-FORM ANSWERS TO THE CIVIL MCT

CIVIL LITIGATION

The reader may be concerned as to whether the questions in this book are of the same length as those appearing in the MCTs set for the Bar Vocational Course. The average length of the questions in the Civil Litigation section of the MCT test set for the students on the Bar Vocational Course in 1994–95 was 166 words per question. Obviously this varies from year to year depending on which questions are used. However, conscious efforts are made to ensure that long questions are balanced by the use of short questions as well. Question 1 in this book is 124 words long, question 2 has 174 words, question 3 has 113 words, and question 4 has 172 words. Of all the Civil Litigation questions set in 1994–95, the shortest was 65 words, and the longest 311 words. In the Civil MCT in this book, the shortest question is number 13 with 80 words, and the longest is question 34 which has 369 words.

1. The first one or two questions in the Civil Litigation MCT are intended to be relatively straightforward. When this question has appeared in the tests it has presented few problems. In order to answer this question it is necessary to have learnt the basic conditions that must be established before the court will consider granting an *Anton Piller* order. These were laid down by Ormrod LJ in *Anton Piller KG* v *Manufacturing Processes Ltd* [1976] Ch 55, and can be found in the **Civil Litigation Manual** at **14.3**. The question asks you

87

to identify the incorrect condition, which is answer [C]. This answer is, to some extent, disguised by the fact that *Anton Piller* orders are in practice most commonly applied for in intellectual property cases, but there is no formal condition restricting the making of these orders to such cases. Some people are prone to make unnecessary mistakes when faced with questions asking for the 'incorrect' answer, so perhaps extra care should be taken when answering this form of question.

2. Under the Civil Procedure Rules (CPR), rr. 10.3 and 15.45 the defendant's obligation to file a Defence or acknowledgment of service arises after service of the particulars of claim (and not the claim form unless it is indorsed with or served with the particulars of claim). In the question particulars of claim have not been served, so the defendant is not in default and consequently the claimant cannot enter a default judgment at this stage (r. 12.3). The correct answer is therefore [D]. Answer [B] has its attractions as Part 8 claims (roughly equivalent to the old originating summons) are outside the scope of judgment in default (CPR r. 12.2). However, a claim for specific performance of a contract will almost certainly raise a substantial dispute of fact, so the Part 8 procedure is inappropriate (see CPR r. 8.1(2)).

3. This is a personal injuries action, so the High Court would be used only if the total award is likely to exceed £50,000 (*Practice Direction 7* (PD7), para. 2.2). An earlier draft of *PD7* stated the £50,000 threshold for High Court personal injuries cases applied to the general damages for pain, suffering and loss of amenities, which would have meant very few personal injuries cases would be brought in the High Court. The final version of *PD7* reverts back to the pre-CPR position of looking at the global sum excluding interest, costs and benefits recoupment, and also excluding contributory negligence unless it is admitted (High Court and County Courts Jurisdiction Order 1991). On the facts, minor bruising is unlikely to exceed perhaps £300, so the total award of approximately £2,500 make this an inappropriate case for the High Court (answers [A] and [C]). As to track allocation, CPR r. 26.6(1) provides that for personal injuries cases the small claims track is the normal track if the total award will not exceed £5,000 and if damages for pain, suffering and loss of amenity will not exceed £1,000. This claim is within both limits, so the normal track is the small claims track, answer [B].

4. This question concerns the interrelation between what are now called Part 20 claims (third party proceedings) and the main action between the claimant and the defendant. As shown by *Stott* v *West Yorkshire Road Car Co. Ltd* [1972] 2 QB 651, in many ways proceedings under a Part 20 claim have a life independent of the main action. However, it is important to distinguish:

(a) Part 20 claims seeking a contribution or indemnity; and
(b) Part 20 claims for substantially similar relief or for the resolution of related questions.

Contribution and indemnity claims brought by way of Part 20 claims against persons not already parties in the case are obviously dependent on the outcome of the claim by the claimant against the defendant. If the claimant loses against the defendant, there is nothing for the third party to contribute towards and nothing to indemnify the defendant against. Therefore, if the claimant's action does not proceed to trial, such as where it is dismissed or struck out in the interlocutory stages, and the Part 20 claim raises only a contribution or an indemnity, there is no reason for the Part 20 claim to proceed to trial, and it will fall with the claimant's action. However, Part 20 claims in category (b) above go beyond reimbursing the defendant for any liability the defendant may have to the claimant, so will continue to trial (if need be) despite the claimant's action being, e.g., struck out or dismissed. In the question Eric has 2 Part 20 claims against George, one in category (a) (the indemnity) and one in category (b) (the damages claim). Hence the correct answer is [C].

5. This question concerns the question of bringing proceedings against a defendant outside the jurisdiction. The proposed defendant is domiciled in France (for which see the **Civil Litigation Manual** at **8.2**, a Contracting State to the Brussels Convention, see **8.2.2**), so proceedings should normally be commenced in France by virtue of Article 2 (see **8.2.3**). The fact the damage was suffered by Marine Fish Ltd in England gives it the alternative of suing in England by virtue of Article 5(3) (see **8.2.5.3**). If it chooses to sue in England, proceedings may be commenced without permission (the new word for 'leave') (see **8.2.1**). Hence the correct answer is [D]. Notice the use of the word 'must' in answers [A] and [B]. There is no need to seek permission under RSC O. 11 (which continues in force by virtue of CPR r. 50(2)), answer [C].

6. Applications for interim injunctions in defamation actions are in an exceptional category and are not governed by the *American Cyanamid* principles where the defendant intends to plead, for example, justification (see the **Civil Litigation Manual** at **12.3.3.4**). Answer [A] is wrong because it outlines the *American Cyanamid* principles. Answer [D] identifies the wrong exceptional category. Answers [B] and [C] both point to the reason (protection of free speech) and the effect of the rule in defamation cases, the difference between them being as to whether the defendant's assertion of an intention to justify can be challenged. As made clear at **12.3.3.4**, an injunction may be granted despite the defendant's protestations if the alleged libel is obviously untrue, so the correct answer is [B].

7. Robert's problem is that he would like to sue the persons responsible for ramming his boat, but he does not know who they are. He believes that Vincent, who is a local person and who was apparently present when his boat was hit, will know who was responsible. Pre-action disclosure (answer [A]) is only available against a likely defendant, so is not available against Vincent as Robert has no cause of action against him. However, a *Norwich Pharmacal* order can be made against such a person for the purpose of obtaining full information as to the identity of the wrongdoer provided the witness got 'mixed up' in the wrongdoing so as to facilitate its commission. The other boat rammed Robert's boat without any help from Vincent, who was merely painting the harbour. Vincent is therefore a mere witness, and the correct answer is [D]. There is no question of self-incrimination on the facts.

8. This question involves the interrelation of two principles in the context of applications for summary judgment. As a result many students have found it quite difficult. The change made by the Civil Procedure Rules from whether there is a triable issue to whether the defence has a reasonable prospect of success should not affect the way these principles apply to the facts of this question. If Peter, the landlord, had sued David, the tenant, simply for the arrears of rent, David would have had a set-off by virtue of his counterclaim for damages for breach of covenant in the lease, see *British Anzani (Felixstowe) Ltd* v *International Marine Management (UK) Ltd* [1980] QB 137 (see the **Civil Litigation Manual** at **10.6.4.4**). As the rent arrears are £6,000 and the set-off is worth £4,000, David has no defence for the balance (£2,000), so the District Judge would have entered judgment for Peter in the sum of £2,000 and given David unconditional leave to defend for the remainder, answer [C]. However, David has given Peter a cheque for £6,000 and dishonoured it. Peter has wisely chosen to sue on the cheque, not for the rent. Under the so-called cheque rule the court will disregard defences and set-offs in relation to the underlying transaction, will enter judgment for the full amount of the dishonoured cheque, and will not even grant a stay of execution (see the **Civil Litigation Manual** at **10.6.4.5**). None of the limited defences to cheque actions listed at **10.6.4.5** applies on the facts of this case, so the District Judge will enter judgment for £6,000, answer [B].

9. In order to answer this question correctly you need to have sufficient knowledge of the special disclosure rules in the Supreme Court Act 1981 so that you are able to identify the correct type of application to make, and you also need to know about the procedure on making such applications. Isaac is suing Highbury: he has no cause of action against the DSS, who hold the documents he wants to see. Being a non-party, it is not possible to seek an order for pre-action disclosure under the Supreme Court Act 1981, s. 33(2) (or its County Court equivalent, the County Courts Act 1984, s. 52(2)). Answer [C] is therefore wrong. An order for disclosure against a non-party may be made after proceedings have been commenced against the defendant (here Highbury) under the Supreme Court Act 1981, s. 34(2) (or the County Courts Act 1984, s. 53), provided the action is one in respect of personal injuries or death. Isaac has contracted a respiratory disease. The statutory definition of 'personal injuries' includes disease (see the **Civil Litigation Manual** at **16.3.1**) so answer [D] is wrong. The difference between [A] and [B] turns on whether the application is made by issuing a separate Part 8 claim (roughly equivalent to the old originating summons) or interlocutory application notice. The CPR rr. 25.1 to 25.3 and 31.17 specify the latter, so the correct answer is [A].

10. Under the old system there were express provisions enabling a court to make orders for further and better lists (answer [B], see the **Civil Litigation Manual** at **15.7.4**); for verification of a list of documents by affidavit (answer [C], **15.7.3**); and for specific discovery (also known as particular discovery, answer [D], **15.7.5**). Under the new system, verification by affidavit has disappeared and is replaced by a general requirement that lists of documents must contain disclosure statements (CPR r. 31.10(5) and PD31, para. 4). As this is incorporated into the list itself, there is no scope for a separate verifying affidavit being ordered on a later occasion. The procedure for ordering further and better lists simply has not been retained by the Civil Procedure Rules. Instead, where a party alleges the other side has given inadequate disclosure, redress may be sought only by seeking an order for specific disclosure (or specific inspection), see PD31, para. 5.1 and CPR r. 31.12. The correct answer is therefore [D].

11. This short question is in fact very difficult. All four answers concern entering judgment in default. Answer [D] contains a common misapprehension that judgment in default can only be entered on the defendant's failure to acknowledge service within 14 days. Under the old system, default judgment could be entered either on the defendant failing to acknowledge within the 14 days, or on the defendant acknowledging within that time but stating no intention to defend: **Civil Litigation Manual** at **9.2.4.2**, para. (b). The answer is still wrong under the new system, because the 14 days runs from service of the particulars of claim (which may or may not be indorsed in the claim form) and because the defendant may avoid having judgment entered by filing a Defence as an alternative to acknowledging service.

The correct answer is [B], which sets out the rule that an irregular default judgment will be set aside as of right (*ex debito justitiae*), as set out in the **Civil Litigation Manual** at **9.5.1** and CPR r. 13.2. The special rule now in CPR r. 12.10, and formerly in RSC O. 13, r. 7B that permission is required to enter judgment in default after service outside the jurisdiction without permission under the Civil Jurisdiction and Judgment Act 1982/Brussels Convention is set out in the **Civil Litigation Manual** both at **8.9**, and at **9.2.4.3**. Answer [A] is therefore wrong because it says judgment in default in these circumstances may be entered *without* permission. The principal question when considering setting aside a regular default judgment is the question of the merits of the defence (see **9.5.1**), not the explanation for failing to acknowledge service (as stated in answer [C]): it is clear that this is merely a secondary factor.

12. Insisting that the applicant merely had to show a serious issue to be tried on the merits was the main point of the *American Cyanamid* decision (see the **Civil Litigation Manual** at **12.3.1** and **12.3.2**). Consequently the correct answer is [A]. Before *American*

Cyanamid the accepted principle was that a party seeking an interlocutory injunction had to establish a prima facie case on the merits of its claim, answer [B]. This often meant the parties felt constrained to attempt to prove the merits of the claim and defence in voluminous affidavits and exhibits, resulting in very long and expensive interlocutory hearings. Avoiding such a waste of resources before trial was the main motivation behind the *American Cyanamid* decision. Answers [C] and [D] are also concerned with the standard of proof, but put the test too high.

13. This is a procedural point in relations to actions commenced by the alternative procedure in CPR Part 8, which is roughly equivalent to the old originating summons. Each time it has appeared in previous MCTs many students have got it wrong. Under the old system the correct answer was [B], see the **Civil Litigation Manual** at **4.2.4**, the obligation to serve evidence being dependent on whether each individual defendant acknowledged service. Under the new system the CPR r. 8.5(2) provides that the claimant's evidence must be filed and served with the claim form, so the correct answer is [A]. The evidence should have been filed at court when the claim form was filed (CPR r. 8.5(1)).

14. Despite the simple form of questions like the present one, they often cause significant difficulties. Before attempting to answer it, it is important to note that it asks for the INCORRECT proposition among the 4 possibilities. Under the Civil Procedure Rules summary judgment is available in all types of cases except residential possession cases and admiralty claims *in rem* (r. 24.3). This cuts down considerably the list of exceptions set down in the **Civil Litigation Manual** at **10.2**. [A] is therefore not the answer to this question. [B] has been the most popular wrong answer (occasionally attracting more candidates than the proper answer to this question). There is nothing to prevent an application for summary judgment for an injunction if there is no defence with a real prospect of success (see *Cadogan* v *Muscatt, The Times*, 15 May 1990, CA). Probably those who selected this answer thought the only way of obtaining an injunction was by trial or on an *American Cyanamid* style interlocutory application. Service of evidence in reply (answer [C]) must indeed be served 7 days before the return date: CPR r. 24.5. PD24, para. 5 makes it clear that the concept of 'leave to defend', whether conditional or unconditional, will not be used under the Civil Procedure

Rules. However, one of the options under the new system is for the court to make a 'conditional order' (para. 5.1(d)), which requires a party to pay money into court or to take a specified step in the action, with dismissal or striking out in default. If the condition is the payment of money, once the money is paid into court the effect is to give the claimant security in the amount paid in (*Re Ford* [1900] 2 QB 211 and **10.6.3** of the **Civil Litigation Manual**), so the money paid in is *not* part of the defendant's general assets on his bankruptcy. [D] is therefore the INCORRECT answer that should have been selected.

15. Dennis must either acknowledge service or file a Defence within 14 days of the deemed date of service of the particulars of claim, otherwise he will be at risk of judgment in default being entered: CPR rr. 10.3, 12.1, 15.3 and 15.4. Answer [A] is wrong because it provides no guard against this. The purpose behind filing an acknowledgment of service is to 'buy' an extra 14 days for filing the Defence (CPR r. 15.4 and notes in the Response Pack, Form N9). (The Response Pack is included in the forms enclosed with a claim form when it is served.) Although the court has power to extend time (answer [B] and CPR r. 3.1(2)(a)) and to stay proceedings (answer [D] and CPR r. 3.1(2)(f)), there is express provision dealing with this situation in CPR r. 26.4. This rule provides that the court will stay the action, initially for a month, for negotiation if all the parties make a request to that effect in their allocation questionnaires or if the court of its own initiative considers a stay would be appropriate. This is in fact the first question in the allocation questionnaire. Therefore, although answers [B] and [D] are not completely wrong, the best answer is [C], which follows the procedure contemplated by the rules for this situation.

16. It is easy to go wrong on this question by not reading it carefully enough. You are asked to identify the proposition that 'best' describes the relevance of the fact the building work has not yet commenced. There are elements of truth in all the answers. Careful reading and a sound understanding of the *American Cyanamid* principles will show that one answer is clearly better than the others. The state of the building work is clearly part of the factual background, but, as will be seen from what follows, it *does* have further relevance to the issues to be considered by the court, so answer [A] is wrong. The court has to consider what the claimant is seeking to injunct and the likely effects on the parties of the defendant's conduct/the proposed order in deciding whether damages will be an adequate remedy, but this is not 'the only relevance' of the fact in question. Answer [B] is therefore an incomplete answer. There is a similar problem with answer [D]. As the work has not started the injunction will be prohibitory. If the work had been completed the injunction would have compelled Lynn to demolish the building, and would have been mandatory. (Different principles apply depending on whether the proposed injunction is prohibitory or mandatory.) Answer [C] is not worded in a restrictive way, unlike answers [A], [B] and [D]. In *American Cyanamid*, Lord Diplock said that where other factors are evenly balanced, it is a counsel of prudence to seek to preserve the status quo (see the **Civil Litigation Manual** at **12.3.1.5**), and hence [C] is the best answer.

17. It is first necessary to identify the nature of the order that has been obtained. Being an injunction restraining Claude from removing assets from the jurisdiction, it is a *Mareva* injunction (now known as a 'freezing injunction'). Note that you are asked to identify the 'best' advice. Answer [A] may have attractions for the dishonest, but would result in Claude being in contempt of court, so is not advice that can be given to him. The Professional Standards Committee would not be impressed if this was your answer! There are elements of truth in answers [B] and [C]. Once a judge learns that the defendant has been notified of the claim, and particularly when the defendant has been notified that the claimant wants some form of security for its damages, the judge may well feel it is inappropriate for *Mareva* relief to be sought without notice. Applications made without notice to the other parties are always exceptional, and the matters mentioned in [B] and [C] may incline some judges into refusing *Mareva* relief without notice. In such cases the claimant is forced into seeking the relief (if at all) after giving notice of the application to the defendant. However, these are not reasons for *discharging Mareva* relief if the judge nevertheless decides to hear the application without notice. The best answer is [D]. *Mareva* relief should only be granted where the defendant is the type of person who would dissipate his assets in order to frustrate any judgment the claimant may obtain (see the **Civil Litigation Manual** at **13.3.4**). Note the rather non-legal phrase used in answer [D] to describe this.

18. In questions like this one it is often useful to compile a short chronology:

September 1992   Accrual of cause of action
July 1998   Service of proceedings
September 1998   Expiry of limitation period
October 1998   Service of Defence
March 1999   Today

It will be noticed that the entry for September 1998 is calculated from the date given for accrual of the cause of action. Richard's proposed amendment is to change the company being sued, and is being sought after the expiry of the limitation period. Generally new parties cannot be substituted after the expiry of the limitation period: Limitation Act 1980, s. 35(3). However, substitution may be allowed after the expiry of the limitation period if it is necessary for the determination of the original action (Limitation Act 1980, s. 35(5)(b)), and substitution may be regarded as necessary if the original party's name was given in mistake for the new party's name (Limitation Act 1980, s. 35(6)(a)). Under CPR r. 17.4(3), which is in substantially the same terms as the old rules discussed in the **Civil Litigation Manual** at **19.7.3.5**, the mistake must be genuine and not such as to cause reasonable doubt as to the identity of the person intended to be sued. Hence the answer is [A]. Answer [C] reflects the general rule in the Limitation Act 1980, s. 35(3), but ignores s. 35(5) and (6). The other answers were all dreamed up for the MCT. Despite the complexity of the above answer, this is a reasonably straightforward question.

19. This question requires knowledge of the bases of taxation of costs. Answer [A] describes the indemnity basis. Answer [B] has been dreamt up, but has its attractions because of the general discretionary nature of costs *orders*. Answer [C] describes the statutory protection on costs of a legally assisted party by virtue of the Legal Aid Act 1988, s. 17. The correct answer is [D], see CPR r. 44.4(1) and (2). This formulation is essentially similar to that discussed in the **Civil Litigation Manual** at **32.14.4.2**, except that under the Civil Procedure Rules the court will also consider whether standard basis costs are proportionate in amount, which is one of the practical applications of the overriding objective in CPR r. 1.1.

20. The old rules on enforcement continue in operation by virtue of CPR Part 50. When answering this question it is first necessary to identify the type of enforcement procedure being described in the answers, and then to consider the mechanics of how they are operated. Answer [A] is the writ fieri facias; [B] is the writ of delivery; and [D] is the writ of possession. All of these are enforced by the sheriff. Answer [C] describes the garnishee order, which, when made absolute, requires a non-party (the garnishee) who owes money to the judgment debtor to pay that money to the judgment creditor. This does not require the intervention of the sheriff. Consequently [C] is the correct answer.

21. Chronology:

November 1995   Julia injured at work
May 1997   Julia consulted solicitors
October 1998   Summons issued
November 1998   Limitation expired
                Negotiations
February 1999   Validity of Summons expired
May 1999   Today

Under the old system (for which see the **Civil Litigation Manual** at **20.2.1** and **20.3**) and also under the new system (for which see CPR r. 7.5(2)), originating process for service within the jurisdiction was and is valid for the purposes of service for an initial period of 4 months.

This case falls within the transitional provisions in CPR Part 51. The claim was issued under the old system before 26 April 1999, when the Civil Procedure Rules were introduced. It is now May 1999. Under the transitional provisions in CPR Part 51 the steps taken to date remain valid (*Practice Direction 51*, para. 10). Any application to extend the validity of a summons issued under the old system must be made in accordance with the new way of making applications (as set out in Part 23), but the court will decide whether to allow the application in accordance with the old law (*Practice Direction 51*, para. 13(3)).

The expiry of the 4-month period of validity (in February 1999) is stated as a given fact in the question. From that basis this question asks what additional advice should be given to the plaintiff, Julia. Answer [A] is to the effect that as the initial period of validity has expired it is too late to apply for a renewal. Under the old system, CCR O. 7, r. 20(2) (which is the same as the High Court rule and much the same on this point to the new CPR r. 7.6) allows an extension to be sought even after the summons has expired provided that there is a satisfactory explanation for the late application (see the **Civil Litigation Manual** at **20.2.2**; **20.3**; **20.4.4** and **20.4.5**). Although it is possible to seek the renewal of the summons, an order should be refused, because negotiations (the reason for non-service in this case) are not regarded as constituting a good reason for renewal (see *The Mouna* [1991] 2 Lloyd's Rep 221 at **20.4.3**). Thus, answer [C] is incorrect. Although the summons will not be renewed, answer [D] is incorrect in saying that a second summons may be issued, relying on Limitation Act 1980, s. 33 to disapply the primary limitation period, which expired in November 1998. The reason is that if a plaintiff (or claimant) commences a first action within the primary limitation period, as here, which comes to nothing, the plaintiff does not suffer prejudice by the effect of s. 11 (imposing the 3-year limitation period) as required by s. 33(1)(a) if a s. 33 order is to be made. The plaintiff's prejudice stems from the failure of the first action. Consequently there is no jurisdiction in such a case to make an order under s. 33: see *Walkley* v *Precision Forgings Ltd* [1979] 1 WLR 606, HL and the **Civil Litigation Manual** at **18.5.3**. Answer [B], which gives the unwelcome advice that the present summons will not be renewed and that the court will not make a s. 33 order, is therefore correct.

22. The requirement that the claimant's cause of action must be justiciable in England and Wales (see the **Civil Litigation Manual**, **13.3.1**) is not of direct relevance to this question, despite the superficial appearance that it is. The question in fact turns on the principles developed by the courts on the requirement that there be a real risk that the defendant in an application for a *Mareva* injunction may dispose of, or dissipate, assets to frustrate any judgment the claimant may obtain, see **13.3.4**. There is no absolute rule that Brussels Convention defendants are immune to *Mareva* relief, and clearly the Supreme Court Act 1981, s. 37(3) and the Civil Jurisdiction and Judgments Act 1982, s. 25 militate strongly against any such argument. Answer [A] is therefore incorrect. There is no requirement as set out in answer [C] for consent from the courts where the defendant is domiciled, whether under the Brussels Convention or elsewhere. The two most popular answers to this question have been [B] and [D]. *Montecchi* v *Shimco Ltd* [1979] 1 WLR 1180 laid down the proposition that it is relevant to take into account the difficulty in enforcing an English judgment in the defendant's country when deciding whether to grant *Mareva* relief. As the **Civil Litigation**

Manual points out, this is of particular significance in relation to EC defendants, because of the ease of enforcing English judgments in other Brussels Convention countries under the enforcement provisions in the 1982 Act/Brussels Convention. The defendant's domicile in a Convention country is not irrelevant (answer [B]), but is a factor to be taken into account as stated in the correct answer, [D].

23. Proceedings may be commenced in England against Daisy Bell only if the rules on seeking leave under RSC O. 11 are satisfied. This remains unaltered by the Civil Procedure Rules: see Part 50. The USA is not a party to the Brussels or Lugano Conventions, so answer [C] is wrong. The fact the claimant is incorporated here does not give the English courts jurisdiction (answer [A]). The facts that the contract is governed by English law and that the English courts have been given jurisdiction provide grounds for granting permission to issue proceedings and to serve outside the jurisdiction (RSC O. 11, r. 1(1)(d)(iii) and (iv)) see the **Civil Litigation Manual** at **8.3.2.1**). Although this is not all that is required (see **8.3.2**), there are grounds for seeking permission, answer [B].

24. Chronology:

3 years ago	Cause of action accrued
7 months ago	Laura served Request for Further Information of the Particulars of Claim
5 months ago	Order to provide the requested Information within 21 days
About 4 months ago	Expiry of the 21 days
	Today
3 years' time	Expiry of limitation period.

Dismissal of an action for want of prosecution (not striking out for abuse of process [C] or discontinuance [D]) on the ground of inordinate and inexcusable delay is part of the court's inherent jurisdiction. As such it ought to survive the introduction of the Civil Procedure Rules. However, on such an application there are a number of conditions, one being that generally the limitation period must have expired. The exceptions to this rule are extremely limited (see the **Civil Litigation Manual** at **24.4.4**). The limitation period is 6 years as this is a breach of contract action, so will expire in 3 years' time. Hence answer [B] is not the practical answer.

One way in which the court may control its procedures and ensure that the parties comply with their obligations under the timetable is by imposing a sanction for breach. It does this by making an order and specifying the consequences for non-compliance. This type of order is often referred to as an 'unless' order in that unless it is complied with the adverse consequences will follow. The court has a discretion whether to make an unless order (CPR r. 3.1(3)). As the order made 5 months ago did not specify any consequences for non-compliance, the next step is to seek an order with a sanction in default (answer [A]).

25. The rules on disclosure of witnesses statements have developed over recent years. The original position was that written statements taken by solicitors from potential witnesses in advance of trial were protected from disclosure to the other side or the court by legal professional privilege, answer [D]. Then, some of the specialist courts within the High Court experimented with mutual exchange of witnesses' statements, answer [A]. Later, rules were made covering all High Court and County Court actions under which the parties could apply for an order (usually on the summons for directions or pre-trial review) for the exchange of witnesses' statements, answer [C]. More recently mutual disclosure was included among the automatic directions which applied in most County Court actions and High Court personal injuries actions. The present position is that mutual exchange of witness statements is one of the usual directions made at the track allocation stage or case management conference, so the correct answer is [B].

26. The rules on appeals (other than the requirement of leave) have remained unchanged by the 1999 reforms (see CPR Part 50). An appeal from a final decision by a County Court Circuit Judge is to the Court of Appeal, answer [D]. See the **Civil Litigation Manual** at **Table 35.1**. For some inexplicable reason students have always had difficulties with this question. Of those getting it wrong, almost equal numbers chose each of the other answers.

27. Mr Brown's report was obtained and paid for by Paul, and has been disclosed to the defendant. A 'better' report has been obtained for Paul from another expert. Having been disclosed, the defendant is entitled to put the first report in evidence: CPR r. 35.11 (the **Civil**

Litigation Manual at **25.10.1** refers to the old rules, which produced the same result), so answer [D] is correct. Before disclosure it was protected by legal professional privilege, answer [C]. Answers [A] and [B] are based on concepts from other areas.

28. You act for the defendant and want to know the nature of other drugs used by the claimant in addition to your client's drugs. An application for specific disclosure (answer [A]) needs to be supported by evidence (see *Practice Direction 31*, para. 5.2) which should specify or describe the documents it is intended to require the claimant to disclose. This might be difficult, as the defendant does not know what drugs the claimant has taken. It would be possible to specify 'all prescription forms', but these will have been given to the chemists, or 'all packaging from drugs taken by the claimant' (which should be held to be documents for the purposes of disclosure), but it is likely that these will not have been retained by the claimant. In any event, if any of the documents are still in her possession they should be in her usual list of documents. The claimant is not a 'non-party' (it is her action!), so answer [B] is nonsense, and without knowing what drugs she has been using there will be no ammunition for cross-examination (answer [D]). The correct answer is [C]. The defendant wants discovery of facts, namely the identities (and quantities) of drugs taken by the claimant, and the service of a request for further information (which performs, among other things, the function previously served by the interrogatories), is the procedure for achieving this. The request will take the form of a list of written questions put to the claimant, which she must answer within a reasonable period. Answer [C] should be the most obvious answer (note, the question asks for the 'most appropriate' advice, rather than the 'correct' advice). The only other answer with any merit is [A]. As the exercise of some judgment is required to answer this question, the other two options ([B] and [D]) have been deliberately designed so they can readily be ruled out.

29. By virtue of RSC O. 114, r. 4 (which continues to apply by virtue of the CPR Part 50), once an order for a reference to the European Court of Justice has been made the English proceedings are stayed until the European Court has given its preliminary ruling on the question referred to it. Rulings given by the European Court are in a general form, so, although the English court is bound by the ruling, it is left to the English court to decide the English proceedings in the light of the ruling of the European Court. Hence the answer is [A]. Answers [B] to [D] were dreamt up for the purposes of the MCT.

30. Where the court makes an order which does not mention costs no party is entitled to costs in relation to that matter: CPR r. 44.13(1). This rule is mentioned a number of times in the *Practice Directions*, with the obvious implication that the court will make use of this simple expedient as one of the possible sanctions against parties who are not conducting litigation in accordance with the overriding objective or in accordance with the ethos of the new rules. The correct answer is therefore [C]. The other answers have simply been made up for the MCT.

31. This question requires the wrong answer to be identified. CPR r. 32.18 provides that admissions pursuant to a Notice to Admit are made for the purposes of those proceedings only (answer [A]). The rule also provides that such admissions shall not be used in favour of any person other than the one who served the Notice (answer [C]). Rule 32.18(4) provides that the court may allow a party to amend or withdraw any admissions made in reply to a Notice to Admit on such terms as the court thinks just (answer [B]). It is a common mistake to think that a Notice to Admit is a means of forcing the other side either to reply or be deemed to admit the facts in the Notice, but the only possible sanction for not replying is in costs (and even this is now relegated to the court's general discretion on costs, as RSC O. 62, r. 6(7) is not directly incorporated into the new rules). See the **Civil Litigation Manual** at **28.3**. The answer to select was therefore [D].

32. On a case management conference the judge will review the steps taken by the parties, decide on the directions that would be suitable, and ensure that all agreements that can be reached between the parties about the mattes in issue and the conduct of the claim are recorded, see *Practice Direction 29*, para. 5.1. To ensure this is a meaningful exercise the parties must ensure that their representatives at the conference are familiar with the case and have sufficient authority to deal with the issues that are likely to arise: CPR r. 29.3(2). This requirement is addressed in the *Practice Direction* at para. 5.2, which goes on to say that where the inadequacy of the representative or his or her instructions (which is the relevant aspect here) leads to the adjournment of a hearing, it is to be expected that a wasted costs order will be made. The correct answer is therefore [D].

33. Where, as here, the claimant sues on 2 causes of action, the defendant has the choice when paying in of making:

(a) a single global payment in respect of both causes of action; or
(b) individual payments in respect of each cause of action.

(See CPR r. 36.6(1), which is in similar terms to the old rules discussed in the **Civil Litigation Manual** at **22.2**.) The defendant has a free choice in the matter, but the Payment Notice must make it clear what the defendant has done. Hence answers [A] and [D] are wrong. When the defendant makes a global payment in (as here), the claimant is generally stuck with it, but is allowed to request clarification and in default of a satisfactory answer can apply for an order that the payment notice be clarified: CPR r. 36.9. The old rules provided that such an application would be granted if the notice was 'embarrassing'. This old fashioned concept has not been carried forward into the new rules. *Pratice Direction 36*, para. 7.3 indicates that the modern test will be whether there is a need for the notice to be clarified. Accordingly, the correct answer is [B].

34. This is the longest question in the Civil Litigation MCT, and is representative of the longer questions that appear on the MCTs. Do not be surprised to find more than one question of this length on any single paper: they will usually be balanced by shorter questions. A careful analysis of the facts is especially important in questions of this type, and setting out a short chronology is an essential first step.

Chronology:

27 February 1993	Cause of action accrued
7 November 1998	Writ issued
December 1998	Defendant's solicitors informed writ issued
6 January 1999	Defendant's solicitors' letter
27 February 1999	Limitation expired
6 March 1999	Writ expired
31 March 1999	Today

This question is set before the implementation date for the Civil Procedure Rules (26 April 1999). If 'today' had been after 26 April, for the same reasons as set out in the answer to question 21, the Civil Procedure Rules transitional provisions treat the writ as effectively issued, and the old rules and principles apply on any application to renew apart from the procedure for making any such application, which must be in accordance with CPR Part 23.

Surprisingly, simply serving and hoping as referred to in answer [A] *is* an option. Serving the writ after the expiry of the limitation period and the expiry of its period of validity does not make service a nullity, but merely an irregularity (RSC O. 2, r. 1 and CPR r. 3.10). A defendant who does not take the point will be regarded as having waived the irregularity. In any event, the plaintiff can apply for the irregularity to be cured (see the **Civil Litigation Manual** at **1.4.3**), even if it will be quite a difficult task to persuade the Court to cure these particular irregularities. Therefore we need to look at the other answers.

It is established that continuing negotiations with nothing more does not constitute a good reason for extending the validity of a writ: *The Mouna* [1991] 2 Lloyds Rep 221, CA (see **20.4.3**). If, being marked 'without prejudice', the letter of 6 January 1999 could not be looked at, answer [C] would be correct. However, such communications are in fact looked at in interlocutory proceedings precisely because they can explain apparent inactivity: *Family Housing Association (Manchester) Ltd v Michael Hyde and Partners* [1993] 1 WLR 354, CA. Answer [D] is wrong because it just considers the need to show a good reason for renewing (here the request to postpone service in the 'without prejudice' letter). On the other hand [B] is correct, because it also considers the need to explain the delay after 6 March, the expiry of the 4-month period of validity of the writ, before applying for the extension.

35. This question concerns the date of knowledge provisions of the Limitation Act 1980, s. 14. In April 1993 William did not know he had been injured. At his medical examination he found out he had a lung injury (which would manifest itself at a later date) which would have justified the institution of proceedings. At that stge he already knew it was due to the chemical escape the previous year, and he always knew the identity of the tortfeasor (his employer). Time therefore began to run in January 1994, answer [B] (or possibly slightly before January 1994, see *Broadley* v *Guy Clapham & Co.* [1994] 4 All ER 439). Knowledge that he had a good legal cause of action, which he obtained after consulting the solicitor (answer [D]), is irrelevant, as expressly provided by s. 14.

36. Like most summary judgment questions, it is easy to go wrong on this question. By virtue of the Sale of Goods Act 1979, s. 53, a defendant being sued for the price of goods sold is entitled to set-off a counterclaim for damages in respect of the breach of the conditions implied by the Act, including the implied term as to satisfactory quality. We are told the facts are not in dispute, so the District Judge will almost certainly act on the facts set out in the evidence. We are told the counterclaim is worth £2,500. Therefore there is no defence to the balance between the price of £4,000 and the value of the counterclaim, £2,500, which means judgment should be entered for Sally in the sum of £1,500. As Brian has a set-off defence to the balance, under the old system he would have been granted unconditional leave to defend for that part of the claim. Under the old system the most likely order would have been 'Judgment for £1,500, unconditional leave to defend for the balance'. The closest answer to this is [C]. Unfortunately, *Practice Direction 24*, para. 5.1 says the orders a court can make on a summary judgment application are:

(a) judgment on the claim;

(b) striking out or dismissal of the claim;

(c) dismissal of the application; and

(d) conditional order.

Paragraph 5.2 has a note which says that the court will no longer follow the former practice of granting a defendant leave to defend, whether conditionally or unconditionally. There is no express provision (unlike the former rules) for granting a stay of execution pending the resolution of a connected counterclaim. So far as this question is concerned, the greatest omission is the lack of anything to indicate how the court should deal with a summary judgment application where there is no defence to part of the claim but a reasonable defence as to the balance. The list in para. 5.1 of the *Practice Direction* could be read as meaning that on a summary judgment application from now on is all or nothing: either judgment for the whole claim,

105

or dismissal of the whole application (albeit with the conditional order for the 'grey area' between the two). Such an interpretation runs counter to the concept of active case management in CPR r. 1.4(2), which is part of the overriding objective provisions, which includes an express provision saying that the court should decide promptly which issues need full investigation and should dispose summarily of the others. Further, *Practice Direction 26*, para. 7.4(2) expressly refers to summary judgment for part of a claim. The best view therefore is that the court can continue making 'split' orders in cases like this one, with the order being similar to the form set out in answer [C].

37. This question needs careful thought. The principles relating to security for costs remain unchanged by virtue of CPR Part 50. The Master has indicated that the defendants' case is marginally stronger than the claimants'. Prospects of success should only be taken into account where one side's case is clearly stronger than that of the other. Otherwise applications for security for costs will degenerate into detailed enquiries into the merits, see *Porzelack KG v Porzelack (UK) Ltd* [1987] 1 WLR 420. Consequently, answers [B] and [D] are wrong. Answer [C] is wrong because the claimant's insolvency is not the only factor to be taken into account. Answer [A] is the best answer because it gets the principle correct on the question of the merits of the respective claims, and also takes into account other relevant factors (defendants' conduct contributing to claimant's insolvency and stifling a genuine claim (the merits of the claimants' claim have to be considered, despite what has been said above, for this more limited purpose)). Notice that the way the Master decides this case (whether to grant or refuse security for costs) does not affect the correctness or otherwise of answers [A] and [D] given the way in which they are phrased. This is inevitable in an area, like this one, where the court has a very wide discretion.

38. Careful analysis is required for this question. You act for the claimant. You have been successful, and want to get your costs from the legally aided defendant. You cannot get your costs from the Legal Aid Board under the Legal Aid Act 1988, s. 18, answer [D], because the proceedings, which were at first instance, were *not* instituted by the legally assisted person (Legal Aid Act 1988, s. 18(4)(b)). [C] is wrong because Martin is protected from the usual costs order by the Legal Aid Act 1988, s. 17. [B] is wrong because the protection is not absolute. The usual order made in these circumstances is that stated in answer [A], which gives the assisted person protection, but allows the successful party to seek leave to enforce the costs order if the assisted person comes into money at some stage in the future. An alternative to [A] was suggested in *Parr* v *Smith* [1995] 2 All ER 1031, namely to order the defendant to pay the claimant's costs, with determination of the defendant's liability postponed for such time as the court thinks fit. The fact that this alternative exists does not make [A] wrong, nor [B] to [D] right.

39. The established safeguards for defendants relating to the execution of *Anton Piller* orders (or search orders as they are called in the Civil Procedure Rules) are set out in the **Civil Litigation Manual** at **14.5.3.2**. A new standard form of order, to be used in all future applications, is laid down in the Annex to *Practice Direction 25*. The supervising solicitor needs to be someone familiar with the workings of *Anton Piller* orders, but there is no need for that person to be a senior partner, and they should not be a member of the firm retained by the claimant (answer [A]). The supervising solicitor is required, among other things, to inform the defendant of his or her right to seek legal advice (answer [C], which is the correct answer), but there is no requirement that the order must be executed in the presence of the defendant's solicitors (answers [B] and [D], the presence of an undertaking to this effect making no difference).

40. Christopher is at the moment the sole defendant. He wishes to make claims against a non-party, Mary, for a contribution towards any liability he might have to the claimant, and he also wants to claim damages in his own right against her. Nothing is said in the question about making his own damages claim against the claimant and Mary, so the possibility of using a counterclaim against the claimant and bringing in Mary as what used to be called a defendant to counterclaim can be ignored (answer [D]). The practice of simply writing to inform a joint tortfeasor that a contribution will be sought (rather than issuing a formal notice to that effect) applies only to joint defendants and where the claim between the existing defendants is limited to seeking a contribution pursuant to the Civil Liability (Contribution) Act 1978. Neither of these conditions is satisfied here, so [C] is wrong too. Although issuing separate proceedings (answer [B]) is a possibility, it is not the only one, and it would be more natural to issue what used to be called a third party notice (now called a Part 20 claim) against the non-party. Answer [B], which uses the word 'must', fails to recognise that there are options, whereas answer [A], which uses the word 'should', does. Further, issuing a Part 20 claim is the sensible option as this has the effect of bringing all the parties to the accident before the court at the same time, removing the risk of irreconcilable findings between the various parties.

CIVIL EVIDENCE

41. [A], [C] and [D] are all exceptions to the rule of finality of answers to collateral questions. As to [A], bias, see, e.g., *Thomas v David* (1836) 7 C & P 350. As to [C], previous convictions, see s. 6 of the Criminal Procedure Act 1865, which applies to civil as well as criminal proceedings. As to [D], physical or mental disability affecting reliability, see *Toohey v Metropolitan Police Commissioner* [1965] AC 595. [B] is an 'invented' exception to the rule – there is no common-law or statutory authority to support it.

42. The general rule governing the incidence of the legal burden in civil cases is that he who asserts must prove. Larry is alleging breach of covenant and therefore he must prove Teresa's failure to pay the rent and clean the windows. Cf. *Soward v Leggatt* (1836) 7 C & P 613, where the plaintiff landlord alleged that the tenant 'did not repair' the house and the defendant alleged that he 'did well and sufficiently repair the house'. It was held that the plaintiff had to prove the alleged breach of covenant. Teresa does not bear a legal burden in relation to the alleged breaches of covenant simply by denying them. However, she does bear the legal burden to prove termination of the tenancy by agreement, because it is a defence which goes beyond a simple denial of Larry's assertions. She is asserting such termination and therefore she must prove it.

43. The general rule as to the incidence of the legal burden in civil cases is that he who asserts must prove. Is Marcus asserting that it *was* reasonably practicable to keep the premises safe, or are 5-X asserting that it was *not* reasonably practicable to keep the premises safe? The identical issue arose in *Nimmo v Alexander Cowan & Sons Ltd* [1968] AC 107, a Scottish civil case in which a majority of the House of Lords held that the defendant employers bore the burden of proving that it was not reasonably practicable to make and keep the premises safe, since on the face of the statute the incidence of the burden was unclear and the court, in determining Parliament's intention, could go beyond the form of the enactment and look at policy considerations and the ease or difficulty that each of the parties would face in discharging the burden. Since 5-X bear the legal burden on the issue, then in accordance with the general rule they also bear the evidential burden on that issue.

44. The common-law presumption of death can only be used to establish the fact of death; if a party wishes to establish that death occurred on a particular date or during a particular period, this calls for specific evidence additional to that required to establish the basic facts giving rise to this presumption. In *Re Phéne's Trusts* (1870) 5 Ch App 139 at p. 144, Giffard LJ said 'the law presumes a person who has not been heard of for 7 years to be dead, but in the absence of special circumstances it draws no presumption from the fact as to the particular period at which he died'. The authorities are in conflict as to the date on which the *fact* of death may be presumed, but that is a different matter.

45. This question concerns the admissibility of similar fact evidence in civil proceedings. The facts of the question are the same, in principle, as those of *Mood Music Publishing Co. Ltd* v *De Wolfe Publishing Ltd* [1976] Ch 119, an action concerning infringement of copyright in which the defendants alleged that the similarity between the work which they had produced and the work in which the plaintiffs owned the copyright was coincidental. The Court of Appeal held that evidence to show that on other occasions the defendants had produced works bearing a close resemblance to other works which were the subject of copyright was admissible to rebut the allegation of coincidence.

46. [C] is incorrect because in civil cases evidence of the character of a party or a witness may be admissible not only when it is one of the very facts in issue, but also (i) if it is of sufficient relevance to the facts in issue (see, e.g., *Hales* v *Kerr* [1908] 2 KB 601 and other civil 'similar fact evidence' authorities) or (ii) if it is sufficiently relevant to credibility (see, e.g., the exceptions to the rule of finality of answers to collateral questions). [A] is well-established. As to the authority for [B], see per Lord Denning MR in *Helliwell* v *Piggott-Sims* [1980] FSR 582, CA. The authorities to support [D] are *Re Bramblevale Ltd* [1970] Ch 128, CA and *Dean* v *Dean* [1987] 1 FLR 517, CA.

47. The Criminal Procedure Act 1865, s. 3, which applies to civil as well as criminal proceedings, provides that a party producing a witness who, in the opinion of the judge, proves hostile, may by leave of the judge prove that the witness has made at other times a statement inconsistent with his present testimony. That party may also ask the witness leading questions: *R v Thompson* [1976] 64 Cr App R 96. However, there is no authority to the effect that a party calling a witness who proves hostile may then cross-examine him on his previous convictions or adduce evidence to show that he is biased against that party.

48. This question concerns the standard of proof appropriate to civil cases in which a party makes an allegation of fraud or criminal conduct. The facts of the question are identical, in principle, to those of *Hornal v Neuberger Products Ltd* [1957] 1 QB 247, CA, where it was held that on a charge of fraud, the appropriate standard is proof on a balance of probabilities, although the court will naturally require a higher degree of probability than that which it would require when asking if, say, negligence is established. Denning LJ said: 'I think it would bring the law into contempt if a judge were to say on the issue of warranty he finds the statement was made, and that on the issue of fraud he finds it was not made.'

49. This question is designed to test your knowledge and comprehension of some of the basic terminology relating to the law of evidence. [C] is the correct answer because if the matter comes to trial, the facts contained in the allegation made by Mane-Line Hairdressers are the facts which they must prove in order to succeed in their defence. As to [A], 'collateral' is used to refer to (i) facts affecting the competence of a witness (e.g., the fact that a witness suffers from a mental handicap) (ii) facts affecting the credibility of a witness (e.g., the fact that a witness has a previous conviction for perjury) and (iii) preliminary facts. As to [B], the adjective 'preliminary' is used to describe facts which have to be proved as a condition precedent to the admissibility of certain items of evidence. As to [D], judicial notice is generally taken of facts which are so notorious or of such common knowledge that they require no proof. The factual allegations made by Mane-Line Hairdressers can hardly be so described.

50. The authority to support [A] is the Children Act 1989, s. 96, whereby a child (a person under the age of 18) who is called as a witness in any civil proceedings but does not understand the nature of an oath *may* be permitted to give unsworn evidence. [D] is well-established: the fact that a witness is compellable will not prevent him from refusing to answer specific questions if he is entitled so to refuse on the grounds of privilege. The authority to support [B], which also illustrates why [C] is incorrect, is the Evidence Amendment Act 1853, s. 1 (together with the Evidence Further Amendment Act 1869). Under these statutory provisions, which reversed the common-law rule to the contrary, a spouse of a party to civil proceedings is competent to testify for or against him.

51. [B] is the correct answer because the presumption of continuance of life is a presumption of fact. On the proof or admission of the primary or basic fact (that a person was alive on a certain date) it *may* be presumed, in the absence of sufficient evidence to the contrary, that that person was alive on a subsequent date – establishing the basic fact does *not* have the effect of placing either an evidential or a legal burden on the party against whom the presumption operates. The presumptions referred to in [A], [C] and [D] are all, by contrast, rebuttable presumptions of law, whereby on the proof or admission of the primary or basic fact(s), and in the absence of further evidence, another fact must be presumed, and the party against whom the presumption operates will then bear the legal burden of disproving the presumed fact or, as the case may be, an evidential burden to adduce some evidence in rebuttal of the presumed fact.

52. [D] is the correct answer, because each statement is admissible as evidence of any fact stated therein of which direct oral evidence by its maker would be admissible: see Civil Evidence Act 1995, s. 1 and s. 6(2), s. 6(3), s. 6(4) and s. 6(5). (The answer was exactly the same under the Civil Evidence Act 1968: see s. 3(1)(a), s. 3(1)(b) and s. 3(2).)

53. As a general rule, answers given by a witness under cross-examination to questions on collateral matters, i.e. matters which are irrelevant to the issues in the proceedings, must be treated as final. [A] is correct (and [B] and [C] are incorrect) because finality, for these purposes, means that the cross-examining party is not allowed to call evidence designed to contradict the answer: the tribunal of fact may or may not accept the answer as true, and the cross-examining party is free to ask further questions about the issue or a related issue. [D] is incorrect because questions on collateral matters are typically questions going to the credit of the witness. His or her answer, therefore, will have some bearing on the issues to be decided by the tribunal of fact.

54. This question concerns proof of an oral hearsay statement. Section 1(1) of the Civil Evidence Act 1995 provides for the admissibility of hearsay evidence in civil proceedings, and references to hearsay include hearsay of whatever degree, i.e., first-hand, second-hand or multiple hearsay: see s. 1(2)(b). Quentin's statement, therefore, may be proved by Quentin, Robert, Sylvia or Timothy. If the employer calls Quentin, however, he may not adduce evidence of Quentin's previous statement without the leave of the court: see s. 6(2). (Under the Civil Evidence Act 1968, [B] was the correct answer because under s. 2(3) of that Act a statement admissible under s. 2 and made otherwise than in a document could only be proved by direct oral evidence from the maker of the statement (Quentin) or any person who heard or otherwise perceived it being made (Robert). Under s. 2(2), if the maker was called as a witness, the statement could not be given in evidence without the leave of the court.)

55. Under s. 31(1) of the Theft Act 1968, questions must be answered in proceedings for the recovery or administration of any property, for the execution of any trust or for an account of any property or dealings with property, notwithstanding that compliance may expose the witness (or his spouse) to a charge for an offence under the Theft Act, but the answers may not be used in proceedings for any such offence.

56. [B] is correct (and [A] and [C] incorrect) because David's evidence constitutes statements of opinion by him on relevant matters (speed, distance, and the suddenness of braking) on which he is not qualified to give expert evidence, all of which have been made as a way of conveying relevant facts. The evidence is therefore admissible under s. 3(2) of the Civil Evidence Act 1972. [D] is incorrect because in civil proceedings admissible non-expert opinion evidence may relate to the ultimate issues in the case – 'relevant matter', for the purposes of s. 3(2), includes an issue in the proceedings in question: s. 3(3) of the 1972 Act.

57. [A], [C], and [D] are all correct. As to [A], the common-law exception relating to public documents was preserved by the Civil

Evidence Act 1968, s. 9(1)(c), and the exception continues to be preserved by virtue of Civil Evidence Act 1995, s. 7(2)(b). The authority for [C] is s. 5(1) of the 1995 Act. (The position was the same under the 1968 Act: the admissibility of hearsay under that Act was subject to the requirement that direct oral evidence by the maker of the statement would have been admissible.) The authority for [D] is s. 5(2)(b) of the 1995 Act. (Formerly the authority was s. 7(1)(b) of the 1968 Act.) [B] is incorrect: see s. 4 of the 1995 Act. (The former statutory requirement was s. 6(3) of the 1968 Act.)

58. The letter is inadmissible for the reasons contained in [C] (not [B] or [D]) because provided that there is some dispute, and an attempt is being made to settle it, the courts are prepared to infer that the attempt was 'without prejudice', even if that expression was not actually used: see *Chocoladenfabriken Lindt & Sprungli AG v The Nestlé Co. Ltd* [1978] RPC 287, a case which also explains why [A] is incorrect.

59. [B] is the best description, because of the Civil Evidence Act 1968, s. 11, which (a) reverses the rule in *Hollington v Hewthorn & Co. Ltd* [1943] KB 587 CA, and (b) operates as a persuasive presumption. Thus under s. 11(1), the fact that a person has been convicted of an offence by a UK court shall be admissible to prove, where to do so is relevant to any issue in the proceedings, that he committed that offence; and under s. 11(2), if in any civil proceedings a person by virtue of the section is proved to have been convicted of the offence, he shall be taken to have committed it unless the contrary is proved.

60. [A] is correct (and [C] incorrect) because legal professional privilege enables a client to claim privilege for, inter alia, statements or reports received from potential witnesses (including experts) provided that the dominant purpose of the preparation of the statements or reports was submission to a legal adviser for use in relation to anticipated or pending litigation. If there was another equally important (or dominant) purpose, for example to inform the client about the cause of an accident so as to prevent such an accident in the future, the statement or report cannot be withheld: see generally *Waugh v British Railways Board* [1980] AC 521, HL. There is no authority to support [B] or [D].

61. There is no authority to support either [A] or [D]. Support for [B] is to be found in *Webster* v *James Chapman & Co.* [1989] 3 All ER 939, ChD, but in *Derby & Co. Ltd* v *Weldon (No. 8)* [1990] 3 All ER 762, the Court of Appeal held that the court is *not* required to carry out a balancing exercise. Dillon LJ said (at p. 783): 'Where the privilege is being restored because the inspection was obtained . . . by taking advantage of a known mistake, there is . . . no logic at all in qualifying the restoration of the status quo by reference to the importance of the document.' [C] is the correct answer: see *Guinness Peat Properties Ltd* v *Fitzroy Robinson Partnership (a firm)* [1987] 2 All ER 716, CA, as qualified in *IBM Corp.* v *Phoenix International (Computers) Ltd* [1995] 1 All ER 413, ChD, where it was held that although the reaction of the actual recipient can be relevant, the question is whether the mistake would have been obvious to a *reasonable solicitor.*

62. [A] is incorrect because provided that an expert states the assumed facts upon which his or her opinion is based, he or she need have no personal knowledge of the facts upon which the opinion is based: see *Beckwith* v *Sydebotham* (1807) 1 Camp 116. Equally, the expert, as a part of the process of forming an opinion, may refer not only to his or her own research, tests or articles, but also to such research and articles etc. by others which form part of the general body of knowledge within the relevant field of expertise: see *Davie* v *Edinburgh Magistrates* 1953 SC 34. [B] is incorrect because in civil proceedings the rule against experts expressing an opinion on the ultimate issues has been abolished by statute: see the Civil Evidence Act 1972, s. 3(1) and (3). [C] is also incorrect: see *H* v *Schering Chemicals Ltd* [1983] 1 WLR 143. For all the above reasons, [D] is correct.

63. The reason why [A] is correct is to be found in *Science Research Council* v *Nassé* [1980] AC 1028, HL, where is was held that there is no principle by which documents are protected from discovery by reason of confidentiality alone but, in the exercise of its discretion to order discovery, a tribunal may take into account the fact that disclosure will involve a breach of confidentiality. The ultimate test is whether discovery is necessary for disposing fairly of the proceedings. If so, discovery must be ordered notwithstanding confidentiality, and in order to decide whether discovery is necessary notwithstanding confidentiality, a tribunal should inspect the documents. A claim to public interest immunity may succeed on the basis of some consideration additional to the confidentiality of the documents, as when the party claiming immunity is exercising a statutory function the effective performance of which would be impaired by disclosure: see, e.g., *Lonrho Ltd* v *Shell Petroleum* [1980] 1 WLR 627, HL. On the facts given, however, no such additional consideration is apparent.

64. An appropriately qualified expert may state his opinion on a matter calling for the expertise he has. The witness is appropriately qualified: expertise may be acquired by experience as well as by study or paper qualifications, and he has been sheep farming in the locality for over 25 years. His evidence is clearly relevant to the issue as opposed to raising any collateral issue. His evidence is evidence of opinion, not fact, whether there is a risk of sheep contracting diseases if grazed on certain types of land, and this is a matter calling for expertise rather than a matter within the experience and knowledge of the judge as tribunal of fact. For all these reasons, [A] is correct and [B], [C] and [D] incorrect.

65. This question provides another factual scenario for application of the principles contained in s. 11 of the Civil Evidence Act 1968. [D] is the correct answer (and [A], [B] and [C] incorrect) for the reasons set out in the answer to Question 59, above.

66. [D] is correct (and [A], [B], and [C] incorrect) because this is a hearsay statement of relevant non-expert opinion admissible for the truth of its contents without the leave of the court. In civil proceedings a witness may give non-expert opinion evidence if made as a way of conveying relevant facts personally perceived: Civil Evidence Act 1972, s. 3(2). Out-of-court statements of opinion satisfying this test are also admissible: s. 1 of the Civil Evidence Act 1995 provides for the admissibility of hearsay statements in civil proceedings and s. 13 of that Act defines a 'statement' as 'any representation of fact or opinion, however made'. (See, formerly, Civil Evidence Act 1968, s. 2(1) and Civil Evidence Act 1972, s. 1(1).) On the facts, there is no requirement of leave. Section 6(2) of the 1995 Act imposes such a requirement only where a party has called or intends to call a person as a witness and seeks to adduce evidence of a previous statement made by that person. (See, formerly, s. 2(2) of the 1968 Act.)

67. [B] is correct because of the well-established rule of public policy that a witness in civil (or criminal) proceedings may not be asked to disclose the name of a police informer: see *R v Hardy* (1794) 24 State Tr 199. [A] is incorrect because confidentiality, *per se*, is not a sufficient ground of immunity from disclosure: see *Alfred Crompton Amusement Machines Ltd v Customs & Excise Commissioners (No. 2)* [1974] AC 405. [C] is incorrect because the only exceptions to the rule are (i) criminal cases in which enforcement of the rule would be likely to cause a miscarriage of justice (see *R v Hennessey* (1978) 68 Cr App R 419, CA, etc. and (ii) cases in which the informer wishes personally to sacrifice his or her anonymity (see *Savage v Chief Constable of Hampshire* [1997] 2 All ER 631). [D] is incorrect because the judge is obliged to apply the rule even if the party entitled to its benefit does not invoke it: see per Lord Esher MR in *Marks v Beyfus* (1890) 25 QBD 494, CCA.

68. Section 10 of the Contempt of Court Act 1981 provides that: 'No court may require a person to disclose . . . the source of information contained in a publication for which he is responsible, unless it be established to the satisfaction of the court that disclosure is necessary in the interests of justice or national security or for the prevention of disorder or crime'. It is a question of fact whether any given case comes within one of the four exceptions, and the burden of proving 'necessity' is on the party seeking disclosure: *Secretary of State for Defence v Guardian Newspapers Ltd* [1984] 3 All ER 601, HL.

69. The statement is admissible under s. 3 of the Criminal Procedure Act 1865, which applies to civil as well as criminal proceedings. It provides that a party producing a witness may, if the witness in the opinion of the judge proves 'adverse' (i.e., hostile), prove that he has made a statement inconsistent with his present testimony. Where such a statement is proved, it is clearly admissible to establish the witness's inconsistency. In civil proceedings, the statement is also admissible as evidence of any fact stated therein: see Civil Evidence Act 1995, s. 1, s. 6(3) and s. 6(5). (See, formerly, Civil Evidence Act 1968, s. 3(1)(a).)

70. The statements in [B], [C] and [D] are all accurate. [A] is incorrect because facts which are beyond serious dispute, sufficiently notorious or of common knowledge will be the subject of judicial notice *without* enquiry. The doctrine of judicial notice after enquiry is used in relation to facts which are neither notorious nor of common knowledge, which is why, under the doctrine, the judge may consult a variety of different sources before reaching a decision. See, e.g., *McQuaker* v *Goddard* [1940] 1 KB 687, CA, where the question being whether a camel was a wild or domestic animal, it was held that books about camels could be consulted and expert witnesses could give evidence concerning their behaviour, before the judge took judicial notice of the fact that they are domestic animals.

APPENDIX 4

NOTE-FORM ANSWERS TO THE CRIMINAL MCT

CRIMINAL LITIGATION AND SENTENCING

1. Since the trial is a summary trial, the answer is contained in the Magistrates' Courts Rules 1981. Rule 13(1) allows the prosecutor to make an opening speech. Rule 13(2) provides that at the conclusion of the evidence for the prosecution, the accused may address the court, whether or not he afterwards calls evidence (so [D] is wrong). Rule 13(4) provides that at the conclusion of the evidence for the defence, the accused may address the court if he has not already done so. Thus, the prosecution have the right to make an opening speech, whereas the defence have the right to make either an opening speech or a closing speech. However, r. 13(5) provides that prosecution and defence may address the Court a second time, but only with the leave of the court (so [A] is wrong and [B] is right).

Note that in a trial on indictment, counsel for the defence can only make an opening speech if the defence intend to call evidence as to the facts of the case other than or in addition to the evidence of the accused: *R v Hill* (1911) 7 Cr App R 1. [C] is wrong because the question states that the trial is a summary trial.

2. Detention without charge beyond 24 hours may be authorised by a superintendent if the offence is a serious arrestable offence; however, the superintendent can only authorise detention for a total of no more than 36 hours from the time of the suspect's arrival in the police station (so [B] is wrong). Detention beyond 36 hours may be ordered by a Magistrates' Court, but only to a maximum of 96 hours, so [A] is wrong (Police and Criminal Evidence Act 1984, s. 45(1)). After the expiry of the warrant of further detention issued by the magistrates, where the suspect has been in custody for the maximum period of 96 hours, the police must either charge him or release him on bail. The suspect cannot be re-arrested for the offence for which he was previously arrested unless new evidence justifying a further arrest has come to light since his release: Police and Criminal Evidence Act 1984, s. 43(19) (so [D] is wrong).

3. Mike is a juvenile; Neville is an adult.

In [A] the adult is charged with aiding and abetting the juvenile to commit an offence (a summary offence, and so the adult has no choice but to be tried in the Magistrates' Court). In such a case, the adult Magistrates' Court may, in the exercise of its discretion, try the juvenile as well as the adult: Children and Young Persons Act 1993, s. 46(1)(b); if the adult court does not try the juvenile it will remit him to the Youth Court for trial.

In [C] the adult and the juvenile are charged with separate, but closely connected, offences. Because the charge against one arises out of circumstances which are the same as or linked with the charge against the other, the adult Magistrates' Court has a discretion to try the juvenile as well as the adult: Children and Young Persons Act 1963, s. 18(b).

As to [D], where it becomes apparent during the course of the proceedings in an adult Magistrates' Court that a defendant who was believed to be an adult is in fact under 18, the court may, if it thinks fit, complete the hearing: Children and Young Persons Act 1933, s. 46(1)(c). If the adult court decides not to carry on with the hearing, the case will be remitted to the Youth Court.

That leaves [B]. The adult and the juvenile are jointly charged with the same offence. The offence is a summary one, and so the adult will have to be tried in the Magistrates' Court. Where an adult Magistrates' Court tries an adult and a juvenile is jointly charged with the adult, the adult court must try the juvenile as well – there is no discretion to remit to the Youth Court: Children and Young Persons Act 1933, s. 46(1)(a).

4. Section 7(3) of the Bail Act 1976 provides that a person who has been released on bail and who is under a duty to surrender into the custody of a court may be arrested without warrant by a police officer if the officer has reasonable grounds for believing that he is not likely to surrender to custody. Thus, [C] is the correct answer.

[A] and [B] are both wrong because the officer did have the power to arrest Tom at the railway station. [D] is wrong because it is irrelevant whether or not the original offence is an arrestable offence.

Note that the question does not ask whether the arrest was in fact lawful; it merely asks what principle is to be applied in determining the lawfulness of the arrest.

5. The charges cannot appear in the same information, as two separate offences are alleged, and so a single information would offend the rule against duplicity (Magistrates' Courts Rules 1981, r. 12(1)). If two or more defendants are charged on separate informations but the facts are connected, the informations may be heard together if the justices think fit. If consent to a joint trial is not forthcoming from all parties, the justices should consider the rival submissions and rule as they think right in the overall interests of justice. The justices should ask themselves whether it would be fair and just to the defendants to allow a joint trial. Only if the answer is clearly yes, should they order joint trial. Thus it is a matter for the discretion of the justices whether the defendants are tried separately or together (*Chief Constable of Norfolk* v *Clayton* [1983] 2 AC 473, at 491–2, per Lord Roskill) and [D] is correct.

6. Criminal damage where the value involved is less than £5,000 must be tried summarily: Magistrates' Courts Act 1980, s. 22. However, such criminal damage is one of the offences to which s. 40 of the Criminal Justice Act 1988 applies (see s. 40(3)). Under s. 40(1), if such an offence is founded on the same facts (or forms part of a series of offences of the same or similar character) as an indictable offence, a count alleging that summary offence may be included in the indictment along with the count alleging the indictable offence (so [A] is wrong).

In the present case, the criminal damage is founded on the same facts as the indictable offence of burglary (since they arise out of a single incident: *R* v *Barrell* (1979) 69 Cr App R 250). [D] is therefore correct.

Burglary is triable either way so Frank can elect Crown Court trial in respect of that offence and [C] is wrong. However, it is a matter for the prosecution whether the criminal damage appears on the indictment – the accused has no right to elect trial in respect of it (so [B] is wrong).

7. Section 6(5) of the Bail Act 1976 provides that an offence of absconding under s. 6 should be dealt with, 'either on summary conviction or as if it were a criminal contempt of court'. In *Schiavo* v *Anderton* [1987] 1 WLR 79, it was held that a Bail Act offence is an offence which is triable only in the court at which the proceedings in respect of which bail has been granted are to be heard.

Frank has been committed to the Crown Court to stand trial. The substantive proceedings will thus be heard in the Crown Court. It follows that the Magistrates' Court has no jurisdiction over the Bail Act offence (so [D] is wrong). In *Schiavo* it was said that the Bail Act offence of absconding is not an indictable offence. It follows that there will not be a jury trial in respect of it (so [B] is wrong). Further, dealing with a Bail Act offence is not one of the situations prescribed in s. 74 of the Supreme Court Act 1981 where a Crown Court judge must sit with lay justices; thus, in dealing with a Bail Act offence, the judge sits alone (so [C] is wrong). [A] states the law correctly.

8. Normally, a person who pleads guilty in a Magistrates' Court may appeal to the Crown Court only against sentence (and not against conviction): Magistrates' Courts Act 1980, s. 108. However, the plea of 'guilty but I have a defence' is an equivocal plea (compare *R* v *Durham Quarter Sessions ex parte Virgo* [1952] 2 QB 1, where a guilty plea was rendered equivocal by subsequent inconsistent mitigation). In such a case, the convicted person may appeal against conviction (so [B] is wrong). The proper procedure is for the Crown Court to decide whether the plea was indeed equivocal and, if it was (as is clearly the case in the present problem) it must remit the case for a trial to take place in the Magistrates' Court: *R* v *Plymouth Justices ex parte Hart* [1986] QB 950. Hence [A] and [C] are also wrong. [D] is correct.

9. There was nothing wrong with the decision of the Youth Court to try Idris as the Youth Court will often try cases which would be tried in the Crown Court if the offender were an adult.

Section 37(1) of the Magistrates' Courts Act 1980 provides that where a Magistrates' Court (in this context, this must mean a Youth Court) convicts an offender who has attained the age of 15 but is under 18 of an offence punishable with at least 6 months' imprisonment, the court may, if it is of the opinion that the offender should be sentenced to a greater term of detention in a young offender institution than it has power to impose, commit him to the Crown Court for sentence. The fact that s. 37 says that the Youth Court may commit the offender to the Crown Court shows that [B], [C] and [D] are wrong. (Note: the position described here may be changed as a result of the provisions of the Crime and Disorder Act 1998.)

10. Section 10 of the Criminal Appeal Act 1968 applies where an offender is sentenced in the Crown Court following committal for sentence under the Magistrates' Courts Act 1980, s. 38. Section 10(2) provides that appeal lies to the Court of Appeal if the Crown Court passes a custodial sentence of 6 months or more, or (inter alia) disqualifies the offender from holding or obtaining a driving licence. As the Crown Court has imposed a custodial sentence of less than 6 months, there is no appeal to the Court of Appeal against that sentence.

11. A juvenile ought to be tried summarily unless:

(i) the charge is one of homicide;
(ii) he or she is charged jointly with an adult who is to be tried on indictment, and it is in the interests of justice to commit both for trial;
(iii) the offence is one of those covered by s. 53(2) of the Children and Young Persons Act 1933 (maximum sentence 14 years or more for an adult, or one of certain specified offences, e.g., indecent assault) and the court considers a sentence under that section might be appropriate. (See the Magistrates' Court Act 1980, s. 24(1).)

Here the only exception to the general rule which might apply in this case is (iii). The stated maximum sentence is such that the offence of burglary of a dwelling falls within the Children and Young Persons Act 1933, s. 53(2).

It follows that [A] is right. [B] is wrong, as the magistrates have a discretion and must themselves decide whether the offences are too serious. [C] is wrong, since a sentence under s. 53(2) would be lawful. [D] is wrong, since juveniles can be tried in the Crown Court for burglary of a dwelling.

12. Summary trials can and often do take place in the absence of the defendant. The Magistrates' Court Act 1980, s. 11 deals with the situation where the defendant fails to appear. It gives the magistrates a discretion to proceed in his or her absence. If they do proceed, a not guilty plea must be entered.

Hence [A] is wrong in its use of the word 'must' since the magistrates are not obliged to adjourn. [B] is right. They do have a discretion to hear the case on the basis of a not guilty plea. [C] is wrong in its use of the word 'must': they have a discretion on the question of whether to proceed. [D] is wrong, since, if they do proceed, they have no discretion as to the plea – they must deal with it on the basis of a not guilty plea.

13. Under s. 36 of the Police and Criminal Evidence Act 1984, the decision to detain must be taken by the custody officer, who should hold at least the rank of sergeant. There must then be periodic reviews of detention – those of relevance here are 6 hours after the original decision and 9 hours after that. The review officer must hold the rank of inspector or above.

[A] is therefore wrong: there was no need to hold reviews at the times stated in that option. [B] is wrong for the same reason. [C] is right, The officer deciding to detain should have been at least a sergeant; the officer reviewing should have been at least an inspector. [D] is wrong, since Jacob does have a legitimate ground of complaint.

14. The procedure for judicial review is contained in s. 31 of the Supreme Court Act 1981, and in the Rules of the Supreme the Court 1965, O. 53. Kevin's first step must be to make an application for leave to apply for judicial review. This is done to a single High Court judge, with grounds supported by an affidavit. It is usually decided on the papers, and is in any event ex parte. Notice to the other side need only be given later, if leave is granted.

Hence [A], [C] and [D] are wrong, since the question specifically asks what Kevin should do *first*, and there is no need to notify the prosecution or the Magistrates' Court at this initial stage. [B] is correct. In the first instance, the application goes to the High Court only.

15. Where a defendant is convicted by the magistrates and appeals to the Crown Court, sentence falls to be reconsidered, even if the appeal is against conviction only. When reconsidering sentence, the Crown Court can reduce it, leave it unaltered, or increase it to the maximum which the magistrates could have imposed (Supreme Court Act 1981, s. 81). The Crown Court can also make such order as to costs as it thinks just.

So [A] is wrong, since the Crown Court has the power to increase sentence. [B] is wrong, since, although the statement as to its powers on sentence is correct, it *can* both increase sentence and order him to pay costs. [C] is correct. [D] is wrong. The power of the Crown Court to increase sentence is limited to the maximum the magistrates could have imposed (6 months for a single count of ABH) and not the maximum applicable to trial on indictment (5 years).

16. [B], [C] and [D] indicate sentences which may lawfully be imposed. A sentence of detention in a young offender institution is available for an offender aged 15 and under 21 years of age whenever the offence is punishable with imprisonment in the case of an adult (Criminal Justice Act 1982, s. 1A). A combination order or Community Service order may be imposed on anyone aged 16 years and over (Criminal Justice Act 1991, s. 11 and Powers of Criminal Courts Act 1973, s. 14). [A] indicates a sentence which cannot lawfully be imposed. A suspended sentence is a sentence of imprisonment which cannot be imposed on a person under 21 years of age (Powers of Criminal Courts Act 1973, s. 22).

17. Where the question of fitness to plead is raised, a jury should decide the issue (Criminal Procedure (Insanity) Act 1964, s. 4(5)). Hence [B] is correct. The flaw in the procedure was that the judge decided on the issue of fitness to plead. [A] is wrong. It is quite usual for the matter to be raised prior to arraignment in this way. [C] is wrong, since a hospital order is one of the orders specified as within the court's powers in these circumstances (s. 5 of the 1964 Act). [D] is also wrong. Fitness to plead can be raised on a murder charge. The distinctive feature in such cases is that if the defendant is unfit to plead, but did commit the *actus reus* of the offence, the only disposition which the judge can make is an admission order to a hospital without limit of time.

18. Where the jury cannot agree, after all appropriate steps have been taken the judge will discharge them, The defendant is not acquitted, and may be re-tried if the prosecution so decide. In practice, it is usual for the prosecution to initiate a second trial. If the jury again fail to agree, the practice is for no evidence to be offered at the start of what would otherwise be the third trial.

[A] is therefore wrong, because it is up to the prosecution to decide and the word 'must' is incorrect. [B] is right. [C] is wrong since the prosecution require no leave to proceed to re-trial. [D] is also wrong, since the defendant has not been acquitted.

19. [A] and [C] are incorrect as the court has no power to impose a custodial sentence and a probation order on the same occasion (*R v Mullervy* (1986) 8 Cr App R (S) 41 and *R v Duporte* (1989) 11 Cr App R (S) 116). [B] is incorrect and [D] is correct for it would be counsel's professional duty to draw the judge's attention to the mistake (*R v Komsta* (1990) 12 Cr App R (S) 63, *R v Nunes* (1991) *The Times*, 31 July, *R v Hartrey* (1993) 14 Cr App R (S) 507 and *R v Richards*, *The Times*, 1 April 1993). See also *R v Stuart* [1993] Crim LR 767, in which a wasted costs order was made against counsel for failing to have the case re-listed within 28 days under s. 47 of the Supreme Court Act 1981 in order that a sentencing error could be rectified.

20. The court can amend an indictment before or at any stage of the trial, unless the amendment cannot be made without injustice (Indictments Act 1915, s. 5). [A] states the law correctly, and is the right choice. [B] is wrong because the counts in the indictment do not need to correspond with those on which the accused was committed for trial, either at the start of the trial or thereafter. [C] is wrong because the indictment can be amended during trial, subject to the limits stated above. [D] is wrong since it is for the court to amend the indictment.

21. This is a case where the guilty plea was entered under duress, and the rules relating to equivocal pleas apply (see *R* v *Huntingdon Crown Court, ex parte Jordan* [1981] QB 857). [A] is wrong since the case will not be reheard in the Crown Court. It will be remitted to the magistrates for hearing on a not guilty plea, as stated in [B], which is the correct choice. [C] is wrong. The magistrates are no longer appraised of the matter and, in any event, the case would not be reheard in the Crown Court. [D] is also wrong, since it is the Crown Court rather than the magistrates which should determine that the case should be heard again by the magistrates.

22. In certain circumstances, the jury can bring in a verdict of guilty of an alternative offence. The general rule is contained in s. 6 of the Criminal Law Act 1967, which states that such a verdict can be returned where the alternative offence is contained, expressly or by implication, in the offence charged. (There are other statutory provisions relating to particular offences, none of which is relevant here.)

[A] is therefore correct. An allegation of robbery includes an allegation of theft, since robbery is theft with additional elements added. [B] is wrong. Theft *is* a less serious offence than robbery, but that is not the reason why the jury can return such a verdict. [C] is wrong because the deletion of particulars can be used to see whether an alternative verdict is *expressly* included in the charge. It does not, however, deal with the other possibility: that the alternative verdict is *impliedly* included in the charge, as it is here. [D] is wrong since alternative verdicts are available in the circumstances specified by s. 6 of the 1967 Act, inter alia.

23. Before or during the course of the trial, counsel may see the judge privately about the case, for example to obtain guidance about appropriate pleas and the likely sentence, provided, of course, that the judge consents to such a meeting. Although many judges refuse to talk privately to counsel about such matters, it is open to the judge to do so. It follows that [B] is an incorrect statement, since it is too restrictive. The Court of Appeal has, however, been anxious to place limits on such discussions, and has stated that both counsel should be present, together with a shorthand writer or a recording device: *R* v *Smith* [1990] 1 WLR 1311. [A] therefore states the law accurately. In order to avoid putting the accused under any improper pressure, the indication given by the judge (if any) must not be conditional on the plea entered, and so [C] is a correct statement of the law: *R* v *Turner* [1970] 2 QB 321. The statement in [D] is similarly consistent with the decisions of the Court of Appeal: where a judge gives an indication, it is in the form of a broad range of sentence, rather than a precise figure. Since the question asks which statement is *incorrect*, it follows that the answer is [B].

24. [A] is correct and [B] incorrect as the maximum aggregate custodial sentence which the Youth Court can impose for 2 or more indictable offences is 12 months, i.e., 6 months maximum per offence to run consecutively, provided that the aggregate term does not exceed 12 months' detention in a young offender institution. [C] and [D] are incorrect as the Crown Court has power to sentence the offender to a maximum of 2 years' detention in a young offender institution per offence, provided that the aggregate term does not exceed 2 years. (See the Magistrates' Court Act 1980, s. 37 and the Powers of Criminal Courts Act 1973, s. 42. Note that the position described here may be changed as a result of the provisions of the Crime and Disorder Act 1998.)

25. An accused whose submission of no case has been wrongly rejected has been deprived of the certainty (rather than the possibility) of an acquittal. The conviction should therefore be quashed, and option [A] is right (see *R* v *Abbott* [1955] 2 QB 497, *R* v *Juett* [1981] Crim LR 113, *R* v *Cockley* (1984) 79 Cr App R 181).

[B] is wrong, both because the accused is entitled to an acquittal, and because the case does not fit within the limited circumstances in which a *venire de novo* is possible (see *R* v *Rose* [1982] AC 822). [C] is wrong, because the accused would have been acquitted if the judge had ruled correctly. [D] is wrong, both for the reasons already canvassed, and because the Court of Appeal will avoid putting itself in the place of the jury.

26. The crucial point here is that the jury have retired. There is an absolute rule that, once the jury have been sent out to consider their verdict, no further evidence may be adduced: *R* v *Owen* [1952] 2 QB 362. The right answer, therefore, is [D].

As to [A], the jury can hear additional evidence for the prosecution if the judge gives leave, but only *before* they retire. [B] is excluded by *Owen*. [C] is wrong: the jury may ask questions after retirement.

27. An appeal against the refusal of bail by the magistrates may be heard by the Crown Court (Supreme Court Act 1981, s. 81), or the High Court (RSC O. 79, r. 9). The second judge should be informed of the first unsuccessful appeal. Hence [C] is right.

[A] is wrong, because no special leave is required for an application to the High Court. [B] is also wrong since an unsuccessful appeal to the High Court does not bar an application to the Crown Court. [D] is wrong in limiting the jurisdiction of the High Court to hear a bail application in this way.

28. Regarding [B], the court when sentencing is entitled to take into account the prevalence of an offence in an area (*R v Cunningham* [1993] 1 WLR 183). Regarding [C], when considering seriousness, it is also entitled to take into account any previous convictions of the offender or any failure of his to respond to previous sentences (Criminal Justice Act 1991, s. 29(1)). The court is also entitled to take into account the need to impose a sentence which is commensurate with the seriousness of the offence as stated in [D] – the 'just deserts' provision in s. 2(2)(a) of the Criminal Justice Act 1991. In *R v Cunningham*, Lord Taylor LCJ said that the phrase 'commensurate with the seriousness of the offence' in s. 2(2)(a) 'must mean commensurate with the punishment and deterrence which the seriousness of the offence requires'. He did, however, go on to say 'What section 2(2)(a) does prohibit is adding any extra length to the sentence which by those criteria is commensurate with the seriousness of the offence, simply to make an example of the defendant'. [A] is therefore the correct answer, as an exemplary sentence would not be permissible.

29. By the Criminal Appeal Act 1968, s. 3, the Court of Appeal may in certain circumstances substitute for the verdict of the jury a verdict of guilty of an alternative offence. The power arises when (i) the jury could, on the indictment, have found the appellant guilty of the alternative offence, and (ii) it appears from the jury's verdict that they must have been satisfied of the facts proving the appellant guilty of the alternative offence.

Theft is an alternative verdict where burglary contrary to the Theft Act 1968, s. 9(1)(b) is charged. [C] is on the facts in this question the likeliest, course of action. [A] is unlikely, since it appears Daniel was guilty of theft, and the Court of Appeal has the power to substitute a conviction for theft. [B] would clearly be a wrong course to take, since Daniel is not guilty of burglary.

It is unlikely that the Court of Appeal will follow course [D]. The evidence for both prosecution and defence indicates that a re-trial will result in a verdict of guilty of theft (rather than not guilty, or guilty of burglary). A re-trial should be ordered only where the interests of justice so require (Criminal Appeal Act 1968, s. 7(1)).

30. Under the Magistrates' Courts Act 1980, s. 38, the magistrates have power to commit a triable either way offence to the Crown Court for sentence, provided that the offender is aged 18 or more, and they are of the opinion that greater punishment should be inflicted for the offence than they have power to impose. They are therefore empowered to commit the most serious of the offences under s. 38. As far as the other offences are concerned, they are able to commit these for sentence under s. 56 of the Criminal Justice Act 1967. This gives them power, when they are exercising powers under s. 38 of the 1980 Act, to commit for sentence in respect of any other offence (summary or indictable) which they have jurisdiction to deal with. It follows that [D] is correct, and all the others are wrong.

31. Whilst the judge is entitled to use a form of words to encourage the jury to reach a verdict, they must not be subjected to any pressure. The case which lays down the form which such a direction ought to take is *R v Watson* [1988] QB 690. In sum, that case approves each of the formulae contained in [A], [B] and [C]. It also expressly rules out any reference by the judge to the unfortunate consequences of a failure to agree, such as cost and inconvenience (overruling *R v Walhein* (1952) 36 Cr App R 167). [D] therefore contains the direction which is forbidden, and it follows that [D] is the correct answer.

32. By proviso (i) of the Administration of Justice (Miscellaneous Provisions) Act 1933, s. 2(2)(a), an indictment may include 'either in substitution for or in addition to counts charging the offence for which he was committed, any counts founded on facts or evidence disclosed in any examination or deposition taken before a justice in his presence, . . . being counts which may lawfully be joined in the same indictment ' It follows that [A] is incorrect.

But the prosecution may not rely on this proviso to prefer an indictment consisting *entirely* of counts in respect of which there has been no committal for trial, even where the accused has been committed for trial on other charges and the offences charged in the indictment are disclosed by the evidence considered by the magistrates (R v Lombardi [1989] 1 WLR 73). That is what has been done here, and it follows that the trial judge's decision was incorrect for the reason stated in [B].

[C] states the law too broadly in view of *Lombardi* and in the light of the words from the proviso quoted above: 'being counts which may lawfully be joined in the same indictment'. [D] is wrong, having no basis in law.

33. The correct answer is [A]. The relevant provision is the Criminal Justice Act 1991, sch. 2, para. 8(2)(b), which provides:

8.(1) This paragraph applies where an offender in respect of whom a relevant order is in force —
    (a) is convicted of an offence before the Crown Court . . .
(2) If it appears to the Crown Court to be in the interests of justice to do so, having regard to circumstances which have arisen since the order was made, the Crown Court may . . .
    (b) revoke the order and deal with the offender, for the offence in respect of which the order was made, in any manner in which it could deal with him if he had just been convicted by or before the court of the offence.

It was held in *R v Bennett* (1994) 15 Cr App R (S) 213 that the Crown Court had no power to revoke a probation order which was not still in force when the offender was sentenced for the later offence. The Crown Court may not therefore revoke the probation order and re-sentence the defendant in respect of the theft offence for which he was placed on probation in 1996, as the probation order is no longer in force. No action can be taken in respect of that theft offence.

34. The *Practice Direction (Crime: Sentence: Loss of Time)* [1980] 1 WLR 663 states that a direction for loss of time in the case of an unsucccessful application for leave to appeal 'will normally be made unless grounds are not only settled and signed by counsel, but also supported by the written opinion of counsel'. The terms of the direction therefore give a measure of protection from such a direction at the stage of application for leave. But no such protection is given where an application has been refused by the single judge, and is then renewed, whether or not counsel so advises. The applicant is vulnerable to a direction in these circumstances. [A] is therefore correct, [B] is wrong. It follows that [C] and [D] are also wrong.

35. The sentence is wrong in law since a defendant cannot be sentenced to a term of imprisonment before the age of 21. The Criminal Appeal Act 1968, s. 11 provides that no appeal shall lie against sentence unless either:

(a) the appellant has been granted leave to appeal by the Court of Appeal; or

(b) the trial judge certifies that the case is fit for appeal against sentence.

[A] is therefore wrong. Arnold *does* need leave to appeal. [B] is incorrect, since there are two ways in which an appeal may lie against sentence, and it is not accurate to state that the leave of the single judge of the Court of Appeal is the only one. [C] is similarly wrong because the certificate of the trial judge is not the sole basis on which an appeal can lie. [D] is correct, as the only answer which properly outlines both alternative routes.

CRIMINAL EVIDENCE

36. [A] complies with s. 8 of the Criminal Justice Act 1967 which, re-establishing the presumption of intention as a presumption of *fact*, provides that the jury, in deciding whether a person has committed an offence – (a) shall not be bound in law to infer that he intended or foresaw a result of his actions by reason only of its being a natural and probable consequence of those actions; but (b) shall decide whether he did intend or foresee that result by reference to all the evidence, drawing such inferences from the evidence as appear proper in the circumstances. None of [B], [C] or [D] complies with s. 8. [D] also erroneously suggests that Gareth has the legal burden of disproving the requisite intent.

37. [B] is correct (and [C] is incorrect) because under s. 10 of the Criminal Justice Act 1967, a formal admission may be made at the proceedings by or on behalf of the prosecutor or defendant, and *R* v *Lewis* [1989] Crim LR 61, CA, establishes that in court, counsel may formally admit a fact under s. 10 *orally*. [A] is incorrect because under s. 10(2)(b) it is if the admission is made *otherwise than in court* that it shall be in writing. [D] is doubly incorrect: the formal admission *is* admissible; and even assuming (wrongly) that it is inadmissible, at common law a judge has no discretionary power to admit evidence which is inadmissible in law.

38. Ghisha, the wife of the accused Fred, is competent to give evidence for the prosecution: Police and Criminal Evidence Act 1984, s. 80(1)(a). She is not compellable because the case falls outside s. 80(3) of the 1984 Act, which sets out the only circumstances in which the spouse of an accused shall be compellable to give evidence for the prosecution. Irene is competent and compellable pursuant to the general rule at common law that all witnesses are competent and compellable. Her position is not governed by s. 80 of the 1984 Act because she is not 'the wife . . . of the accused' – her husband, Harry, by pleading guilty, has ceased to be an accused.

39. [A] is incorrect because although in a summing-up a judge should not attempt any gloss upon the meaning of 'reasonable doubt', because it is more likely to confuse than help the jury, in exceptional cases, as when the jury return to court and ask for a further direction, the jury should be given help: see *R* v *Yap Chuan Ching* (1976) 63 Cr App R 7, CA. The direction in [B] has been expressly disapproved: *R* v *Stafford* and *R* v *Luvaglio* (1968) 53 Cr App R 1. The direction in [C] suggests too low a standard of proof: *R* v *Gray* (1973) 58 Cr App R 177. The direction in [D] was upheld by the Privy Council in *Walters* v *R* [1969] 2 AC 26.

40. [A] is incorrect because even if the evidence of discovery of the magazines could be said to show Michael's disposition to commit the kind of offence with which he is charged – which it does not – it would be inadmissible under Lord Herschell's first proposition in *Makin* v *Attorney-General for New South Wales* [1894] AC 57, PC. See also per Neill LJ in *R* v *Lunt* (1987) 85 Cr App R 241, CA, at p. 245. [B] is incorrect: if Michael's defence was that he had touched Nora accidentally, there might be a case for a submission that the evidence goes to rebut it, but the evidence clearly does not rebut a mere denial – see *R* v *Lewis* (1983) 76 Cr App R 33 and *R* v *B (RA)* [1997] 2 Cr App R 88. [D] is incorrect because however relevant this evidence may be – and views may differ – it is certainly not 'highly' relevant. As to [C], the correct answer, the evidence in this case does not have sufficiently probative value to outweigh its obvious prejudicial effect.

41. Under s. 2(2) of the Homicide Act 1957, an express statutory exception to the general rule laid down in *Woolmington* v *DPP* [1935] AC 462, HL, the accused bears the legal burden of establishing the defence of diminished responsibility on a charge of murder. The defence will also bear the evidential burden, in accordance with the general rule that a party bearing the legal burden on an issue will also bear the evidential burden on that issue. Where the legal burden on an issue is borne by the accused, it is discharged by proof on a balance of probabilities: see *R* v *Carr-Briant* [1943] KB 607, CCA and *R* v *Dunbar* [1958] 1 QB 1.

42. The facts of this case are, in principle, identical to those of *R* v *Burke* (1858) 8 Cox CC 44. In that case an Irish witness gave evidence through an interpreter and was cross-examined about his knowledge of English. He denied that he could speak English. It was held that evidence in rebuttal was inadmissible under the rule of finality of answers to questions concerning collateral matters, because his ability to speak English was irrelevant to the matters directly in issue in the case. For this reason, [C] is correct and [A], [B] and [D] incorrect. As to [D], it should be added, it has been said that *where the disputed issue is a sexual one between two persons in private*, the difference between questions going to credit and questions going to the issue is reduced to vanishing point: see per Henry J in *R v Funderburk* [1990] 2 All ER 482, CA, at p. 491.

43. (i) is possible under s. 10 of the Criminal Justice Act 1967. (ii) is possible under s. 6 of the Criminal Procedure Act 1865 and s. 73 of the Police and Criminal Evidence Act 1984. As to (iii), the situation is not governed by s. 1(f) of the Criminal Evidence Act 1898. Section 1(f) begins: 'A person charged and called as a witness . . .', but Tom does not give evidence. Thus if the accused does not testify and the defence cross-examine a prosecution witness as to his bad character, but do not adduce evidence as to the accused's good character and do not cross-examine prosecution witnesses with a view to establishing the accused's good character, evidence of the accused's bad character may not be called for the prosecution; the accused has not put his own character in issue, but that of the prosecution witness – see *R v Butterwasser* [1948] 1 KB 4, CCA.

44. The statement in (i) is correct because the general rule is that a witness may not be asked in examination-in-chief about former statements made by him and consistent with his evidence in the proceedings: see *R v Roberts* [1942] 1 All ER 187. The statement in (ii) is correct because one of the exceptions to the general rule arises if, in cross-examination, it is suggested to the witness that his version of events is a recent invention or fabrication, in which case evidence of a prior statement to the same effect will be admissible, in re-examination, to support his credit: see, e.g., *R v Oyesiku* (1971) 56 Cr App R 240, CA.

45. [A] is incorrect because previous identification of the accused is a well-established exception to the general rule against previous consistent or self-serving statements. [B] is incorrect (and [D] correct) because it is generally undesirable and improper first to invite a witness to identify the accused from the witness-box, i.e., to make a 'dock identification' (see *R v Cartwright* (1914) 10 Cr App R 219); if there has been a previous out-of-court identification of the accused by the witness, the best and usual practice is to elicit evidence of the previous identification *before* then asking the witness whether that person is in the court-room. [C] is incorrect because if the witness cannot give evidence identifying the accused in court, there is no testimony with which the previous identification can be consistent.

46. [B] is incorrect because the evidence is clearly relevant to the issue whether Alf's conduct was deliberate or accidental. There is no authority to support [D]. [C] is the correct answer (and [A] incorrect) because the evidence may be admitted on the same reasoning employed in (i) 'similar fact' cases such as *Makin* v *Attorney-General for New South Wales* [1894] AC 57, PC, and *R* v *Smith* (1915) 11 Cr App R 229, CCA (given the defence, the magnitude of the coincidence involved) or *DPP* v *Boardman* [1975] AC 421, HL (evidence so very relevant that to exclude it would be an affront to common sense) or (ii) *R* v *P* [1991] 3 All ER 337, HL (the evidence of the victims is so related that the evidence of the first provides strong enough support for the evidence of the second to make it just to admit it notwithstanding its prejudicial effect).

47. Harriet is competent to give evidence for the prosecution: Police and Criminal Evidence Act 1984, s. 80(1)(a). She is not compellable, however, because the case falls outside s. 80(3) of the 1984 Act, which sets out the only circumstances in which the spouse of an accused shall be compellable to give evidence for the prosecution. Kenneth is competent to give evidence for Julia: s. 80(1)(b) of the 1984 Act. He is also compellable: s. 80(2) of the 1984 Act. For these reasons, [C] is correct and [A], [B] and [D] are incorrect.

48. Michelle is competent for the prosecution under s. 80(1)(a) of the Police and Criminal Evidence Act 1984, and compellable for the prosecution under both parts of s. 80(3)(a) of the 1984 Act ('the offence charged involves an assault on . . . the wife . . . of the accused or a person who was at the material time under the age of 16'). For these reasons, [B] is correct (and [A], [C] and [D] incorrect). As to [A], the fact that Michelle is separated from John makes no difference: they are still married. Even if they were no longer married, the answer would be the same, because a person who is no longer married to the accused shall be competent and compellable to give evidence as if that person and the accused had never been married: s. 80(5) of the 1984 Act.

49. As to [A], there is no authority to suggest that an accused may be cross-examined on previous convictions if 'not a credible witness'. As to [B], Morgan could be cross-examined on his previous convictions if he had cast imputations on the character of a prosecution witness (under s. 1(f)(ii) of the Criminal Evidence Act 1898), but on the facts given no such imputation has been cast. [C] is correct because the words 'to show' in s. 1(f) of the 1898 Act mean 'to make known', 'to reveal' or 'to disclose', and therefore cross-examination will not be prohibited because the jury are already aware of the fact that he has been in trouble with the police before: *Jones* v *DPP* [1962] AC 635. [D] is incorrect because even if the previous conviction could be said to show Morgan's general propensity towards offences of a sexual nature, it would be inadmissible under Lord Herschell's first proposition in *Makin* v *Attorney-General for New South Wales* [1894] AC 57, PC.

50. [B] is correct: see *R* v *Vye* [1993] 1 WLR 471, CA. (The accused is not entitled to a direction on the relevance of the evidence of good character to his *credit*, because he is relying on a wholly exculpatory statement, not a 'mixed' statement: see *R* v *Aziz* [1995] 3 All ER 149, HL.) [A] is incorrect: at common law, evidence of bad character may also be admitted, in appropriate circumstances, as similar fact evidence. [C] is incorrect because 'character' as used in s. 1(f) of the Criminal Evidence Act 1898 refers to disposition as well as reputation: *R* v *Dunkley* [1927] 1 KB 323, CCA. [D] is incorrect: see s. 1(e) of the 1898 Act and *Jones* v *DPP* [1962] AC 635, HL.

51. [B] is correct (and [A] incorrect) because the statement is in a document; the statement contains facts of which direct oral evidence would be admissible; the document was created by David in the course of his occupation; and the information contained in the document was supplied to him by a person, David himself, who had personal knowledge of the matters dealt with (s. 24(1)). If the statement was prepared for the purposes of a criminal investigation, then it would be necessary to satisfy the requirements of s. 24(4): on the facts given, the requirement in s. 24(4)(iii) would be satisfied (maker cannot be expected to have any recollection). The statement is only admissible 'in principle' because of the discretion to exclude under s. 25 of the 1988 Act. [C] is incorrect because there is nothing to satisfy the requirements of one of the paragraphs of s. 23(2) or the requirements of s. 23(3). [D] is incorrect because there is nothing on the facts to suggest that the statement is admissible for some relevant purpose other than the truth of its contents.

52. The out-of-court statement allegedly made by Amanda is admissible hearsay: it is a confession as defined in the Police and Criminal Evidence Act 1984, s. 82(1) ('any statement . . . adverse to the person who made it') and admissible under s. 76(1) of that Act. Concerning a voir dire, where the prosecution intend to rely on an oral confession and the defence case is simply that the accused never made it, no question of admissibility arises for the judge to decide and there is therefore no need for a voir dire; the only issue is a question of fact, whether or not the accused made the confession, and that is for the jury: see *Ajodha* v *The State* [1981] 2 All ER 193, PC, applied in *R* v *Flemming* (1988) 86 Cr App R 32, CA. It would be otherwise, of course, had Amanda alleged oppression, something said or done likely to render unreliable any consequent confession, or some impropriety (apart from the alleged invention of the confession).

53. [D] is correct (and [A] incorrect) because the statement was made in a document; the statement contains facts of which direct oral evidence would be admissible; and the person who made it is dead (Criminal Justice Act 1988, s. 23(1) and (2)(a)). Subject to the discretion to exclude under s. 25 of that Act, it is therefore admissible hearsay. [B] is incorrect because the document was not created or received by a person in the course of a trade, business, profession etc. (s. 24(1)(i)). [C] is incorrect because a dying declaration is admissible only if, inter alia, (i) it relates to the cause of the victim's injuries and (ii) at the time when it was made, the victim was under a settled hopeless expectation of death.

54. [A] is correct (and [C] incorrect) because of the decision in *DPP* v *Marshall* [1988] 3 All ER 683, DC, where on a charge of selling intoxicating liquor without a licence, it was held that evidence of purchases by plain clothes officers was admissible. [B] is incorrect because of the very wording of s. 78 of the Police and Criminal

Evidence Act 1984: 'if it appears to the court that, having regard to all the circumstances, including the circumstances in which the evidence was obtained . . .'. Concerning [D], see *R* v *Christou* [1992] QB 979, CA. In that case, it was held that Code C (which includes the requirement to caution) is intended to protect suspects who are, or may believe themselves to be, vulnerable to abuse or pressure from officers acting as such. Although it was also held that it would be wrong for the police to adopt an undercover pose to enable them to ask questions about an offence uninhibited by the Code and with the effect of circumventing it (in which case, a judge could exclude under s. 78), on the facts the officers' questions were not about the offence but, for the most part, simply necessary to maintain their cover. Cf. *R* v *Bryce* [1992] 4 All ER 567, CA.

55. [A] is incorrect because the conditions of admissibility contained in s. 76 apply to a 'confession' and this is defined to include 'any statement . . . whether made to a person in authority or not' (s. 82(1) of the 1984 Act). [B] is incorrect because under s. 76(2)(b) the judge may only rule a confession admissible if, 'notwithstanding that it may be true', he is satisfied beyond reasonable doubt that it was not obtained in consequence of anything done or said etc. [C] is correct: s. 76(2)(b) requires a causal connection between what was said or done and the confession. Thus if the judge was satisfied that the confession was not obtained 'in consequence of Beatrice's statement', this could have been the justification for his decision to admit it. There is no authority to support [D].

56. [B] is correct because where, at a trial on indictment, the case against the accused depends wholly or substantially on a confession by him and the court is satisfied that (i) he is mentally handicapped and (ii) the confession was not made in the presence of an independent person, the court shall warn the jury that there is a special need for caution: see the Police and Criminal Evidence Act 1984, s. 77. There is no authority to support [A]. [C] is incorrect: there is no common-law or statutory authority to permit a mentally-handicapped person to give his or her evidence *unsworn*. [D] is incorrect because the proper test of the competence of a mentally-handicapped person is not whether he or she understands the divine sanction of the oath, but the secular test adopted (in the case of children) in *R* v *Hayes* [1977] 1 WLR 234: see *R* v *Bellamy* (1985) 82 Cr App R 222, CA.

57. [D] is correct (and [A] and [C] incorrect) because of the ruling of the Court of Appeal in *R v Cook* [1987] 1 All ER 1049, that photofits, together with sketches and photographs, are in a class of their own to which neither the rule against hearsay nor the rule against previous consistent statements is applicable. On the particular facts, see also *R v Dodson*; *R v Williams* (1984) 79 Cr App R 220, CA, where it was held that photographs taken by security cameras installed at a building society office at which an armed robbery was attempted, were admissible, being relevant to the issues of whether an offence was committed and, if so, who committed it. [B] is incorrect because although a document, for the purposes of the Criminal Justice Act 1988, s. 24, is defined to include a photograph (sch. 2, para. 5 of the 1988 Act), it is difficult to see how the information contained in the photograph could sensibly be said to have been 'supplied by a person . . . who had . . . personal knowledge of the matters dealt with'.

58. [B] is correct because the statement was made in a document; the statement contains facts of which direct oral evidence would be admissible; and its maker is dead (Criminal Justice Act 1988, s. 23(1) and (2)(a)). [A] is incorrect because the Police and Criminal Evidence Act 1984, s. 76, which governs the admissibility of confessions in criminal cases, only admits 'a confession made by an accused person' (s. 76(1)). [C] is incorrect because the statement was clearly not made in circumstances of such spontaneity or involvement in the event, i.e., the murder, that the possibility of concoction can be disregarded: see *Ratten* v *R* [1972] AC 378, PC etc. [D] is incorrect because a dying declaration is admissible at a trial for murder or manslaughter only if, inter alia, it was made by the victim and relates to the cause of his or her injuries.

59. [B] is correct because the statement is admissible original evidence, i.e., evidence tendered for a relevant purpose other than proving the truth of the facts it contains, namely to show what Robin, who heard it, thought or believed, which has an obvious relevance to his defence: cf. *Subramaniam* v *Public Prosecutor* [1956] 1 WLR 965. [A] is incorrect because the event in question, the purchase of a video, can hardly be said to have been so unusual, startling or dramatic as to have dominated the thoughts of the neighbour and given him or her no real opportunity for reasoned reflection: see per Lord Ackner in *R* v *Andrews* [1957] 1 All ER 513, HL, at pp. 520–1. [C] is incorrect because the statement, if tendered for the truth of its contents, will be inadmissible hearsay. [D] is incorrect because the Criminal Justice Act 1988, s. 23, only admits statements made by a person 'in a document'.

60. In *R* v *Goodway* [1993] 4 All ER 894, CA, it was held that a *Lucas* direction should be given, save where it is otiose, whenever lies are or may be relied on in support of prosecution evidence of the accused's guilt, and not merely in corroboration and identification cases. In *R* v *Lucas* [1981] QB 720, it was held that to be capable of amounting to corroboration (i) the lie must be deliberate (ii) it must relate to a material issue (iii) the motive for it must be a realisation of guilt and a fear of the truth and (iv) it must clearly be shown to be a lie by admission or by evidence from an independent witness, i.e., a witness other than the witness requiring corroboration or a warning. There is no requirement that the lie should be in writing or otherwise recorded in documentary form.

61. (1) is incorrect because a confession may be excluded under the Police and Criminal Evidence Act 1984, s. 76(2)(b) where there is not even a suspicion of impropriety: see per Lord Lane CJ in *R* v *Fulling* [1987] 2 All ER 65, CA and, e.g., *R* v *Harvey* [1988] Crim LR 241, CC. (2) is correct because the test of reliability under s. 76(2)(b) is hypothetical, in the sense that on its very wording it applies to 'any confession' which might be made by the accused: see *R* v *Barry* (1991) 95 Cr App R 384, CA.

62. (1) is incorrect, because under the Police and Criminal Evidence Act 1984, s. 76(2), the defence may raise the question of admissibility merely by making a 'representation' to the court that the confession was or may have been obtained by the methods described – the holding of a voir dire is thus not conditional upon evidence in support of such a representation. (2) is incorrect because under s. 76(2), a confession obtained by oppression will be excluded 'notwithstanding that it may be true'.

63. [C] is correct (and [A] incorrect) because the statement is in a document; the statement contains facts of which direct oral evidence would be admissible; the document was created by Luke in the course of his occupation; the information contained in the document was supplied to him by Jim, who had personal knowledge of the matters dealt with; and the statement having been prepared for the purposes of a criminal investigation, Luke is dead (s. 24(1) and (4)). It seems that the requirement in s. 24(4) that the maker of the statement be unable to attend or testify for one of the specified reasons applies to the person who actually made the statement and not to the person who supplied the information contained in it: *Brown v Secretary of State for Social Security* (1994) *The Times*, 7 December, DC. The statement is only admissible 'in principle' because of the requirement of leave under s. 26 and the discretion to exclude under s. 25. [B] is incorrect because s. 23 applies only to first-hand documentary hearsay and Jim has not 'made a statement in a document' – he did not read and sign the document nor check that what Luke had written down was an accurate record of what he had said: *R v McGillivray* (1993) 97 Cr App R 232, CA. [D] is incorrect because, among other reasons, (a) Jim, not Luke, made the 'declaration' and (b) under that common-law exception to the hearsay rule, the declaration must relate to an act performed by the deceased, and not by another or others: *The Henry Coxon* (1878) 3 PD 156.

64. [A] is correct because the out-of-court statement is being tendered for the truth of its contents but is not covered by any exception to the rule against hearsay. [B] is incorrect because s. 23 applies only to first-hand documentary hearsay: see the answer to Question 63, above. [C] is incorrect because the information contained in the document created by Luke was supplied indirectly, but the person through whom it was supplied, Ken, did not receive it in the course of a trade, business, profession etc. (s. 24(2)). [D] is incorrect because, among other reasons, under that common-law exception to the hearsay rule, the record must be compiled by a person acting under a public duty to record findings so that the public may refer to them: see, e.g., *Lilley v Pettit* [1946] KB 401, DC.

65. [C] is correct (and [A] and [B] incorrect) because in *R v Turnbull* [1977] QB 224, Lord Widgery CJ held that whenever the case against an accused depends wholly or substantially on the correctness of one or more identifications of the accused, which the defence allege to be mistaken, and in the judgment of the judge the quality of the identifying evidence is poor, he or she should direct an acquittal unless there is other evidence, which need not be corroboration in the strict sense, which goes to support the correctness of the identification. As to [D], a judge should not direct a jury that he would have withdrawn the case from them had he thought that there was insufficient identification evidence, because the jury may thereby mistakenly conclude that the evidence is sufficiently strong for them to convict: see *R v Smith and Doe* (1986) 85 Cr App R 197, CA and *R v Akaidere* [1990] Crim LR 808, CA.

66. [A] is correct (and [C] and [D] incorrect) because if a man admits something of which he knows nothing, it is of no real evidential value: see *Comptroller of Customs v Western Electric Co. Ltd* [1966] AC 367, PC, where an admission as to the country of origin of imported goods, made in reliance on marks and labels borne by the goods, was held to be evidentially worthless. The suggestion in [B] that the admissions may be admissible not for the truth of their contents, but as original evidence, i.e., simply to show that the statements were made, is incorrect: an out-of-court statement is only admissible as original evidence if it serves some relevant purpose other than that of proving the truth of the facts it contains but, on the facts given, there is no such relevant purpose.

67. The facts clearly fall within the Criminal Justice and Public Order Act 1994, s. 34(1): evidence has been given that Adam, on being charged with the offence, failed to mention any of the facts relied on in his defence, being facts which, the parties agree, in the circumstances existing at the time he could reasonably have been expected to mention when charged. Therefore s. 34(2) applies and the statements in (i) and (ii) are both accurate: see s. 34(2)(c) and (d) respectively. The statement in (iii) is also accurate: see s. 38(3).

68. [D] is correct (and [A], [B] and [C] incorrect) because where the jury can form their own opinion about a particular matter without the assistance of an expert, that matter being within their own knowledge and experience, expert opinion evidence is inadmissible because unnecessary: per Lawton LJ in *R v Turner* [1975] QB 834 at p. 841. Thus expert psychiatric evidence is generally inadmissible on the question of *mens rea*, credibility, provocation or the reliability of a confession (although it is a practical necessity in order to establish insanity or diminished responsibility, and will be admissible on the question of *mens rea* or the reliability of a confession if the accused comes into the class of mental defective). Compare the facts with those of *R* v *Turner*, ibid.

69. [B] is correct (and [C] and [D] are incorrect) because under the Police and Criminal Evidence Act 1984, s. 67(9), the Codes apply not only to police officers, but also to other persons 'charged with the duty of investigating offences or charging offenders'; and whether a person satisfies this test is a question of fact in each case (per Watkins LJ in *R* v *Seelig* [1991] 4 All ER 429, CA, at p. 439) or, more accurately, a question of mixed law and fact, involving an examination of the statute, contract or other authority under which a person carries out his functions, as well as a consideration of his actual work (*R* v *Bayliss* (1994) 98 Cr App R 235, CA and *R* v *Smith* (1994) 99 Cr App R 233, CA). As to [A], Naomi's questioning could have been an interview, which is defined as the questioning of a person regarding his involvement or suspected involvement in a criminal offence which is required to be carried out under caution: see sections 10.1 and 11, Code C.

70. The facts of the case fall within the Criminal Justice and Public Order Act 1994, s. 36(1)(a) and (b): the arresting officer reasonably believed that the condition of the clothing (see s. 36(3)) was attributable to George's participation in the commission of the offence, and he informed George of his belief and asked him to account for the condition of his clothing, but George refused to do so. Prima facie, therefore, (a) the court, in deciding whether there is a case to answer, and (b) the court or jury, in deciding whether the accused is guilty of the offence charged, may draw proper inferences from the refusal: s. 36(2). However, s. 36(4) provides that s. 36(1) and (2) do not apply unless the accused was told in ordinary language by the constable, when making the request, what the effect would be if he failed or refused to comply with it.

APPENDIX 5

CIVIL LITIGATION SYLLABUS

High Court and County Court jurisdiction.
Computation of time and non-compliance with Rules of Court.
Commencement in the County Court including types of proceedings.
Commencement in the High Court.
Statements of case and Service.
Parties, joinder, representative actions, consolidation of actions, intervening, interpleader.
Third party (Part 20) procedure and contribution notices.
Procedure on interim applications.
Service outside the jurisdiction with and without permission.
Judgments in default in the High Court and County Court.
Summary judgments in the High Court and County Court and interim payments.
Interim injunctions, *Mareva* injunctions (freezing orders) and *Anton Piller* orders (search orders).
Disclosure and inspection of documents.
Norwich Pharmacal orders; pre-action disclosure under SCA 1981, s. 33(2); disclosure against non-parties under SCA 1981, s. 34(2); orders for the inspection of property including orders under SCA 1981, s. 34(3) and SCA 1981, s. 33(1); interim delivery up of goods.
Requests for further information.
Limitation.
Amendment of process including amendment after the expiry of the limitation period.
Renewal of process.
Security for costs.
Payments into court and *Calderbank* letters (Part 36 payments and Part 36 offers).
Provisional damages.

Directions, track allocation and case management.
Striking out, sanctions, dismissal for want of prosecution, stays, discontinuance.
Experts, including obtaining facilities for examination, directions, exchange of reports, procedure at trial.
Witnesses statements including exchange and procedure at trial.
Hearsay in civil proceedings including hearsay notices.
Notices to admit and notices to produce.
Listing for trial.
Preliminary issues, witnesses, trial procedure.
References to the European Court.
Legal aid and costs.
Judgments, consent orders, *Tomlin* orders, unless orders (in outline only).
Enforcement (in outline only).
Appeals (in outline only).

CRIMINAL LITIGATION AND SENTENCING SYLLABUS

Preliminary Matters

Police powers of arrest; detention at a police station under the Police and Criminal Evidence Act; access to legal advice; Codes of Practice issued under PACE 1984; 'serious arrestable offences'; charges; issue of process at Magistrates' Courts; legal aid.

Remands and Bail

Distinguishing between simple adjournments and remands; situations where a remand must be used; duration of remands; general right to bail; attaching conditions to release on bail; sureties and forfeiture; applying for bail; limit on number of applications; appeals to or variations by a judge (of the High Court or Crown Court); custody time limits.

Mode of Trial

Classification of offences; determination of mode of trial including the plea before venue procedure; special provisions for criminal damage; advance information; Criminal Justice Act 1988, ss. 40 and 41.

Summary Trial

Procedure at trial of a charge or summons; joint trial of separate informations; proceeding in the accused's absence; guilty pleas by post; committals for sentence to the Crown Court (under the Magistrates' Courts Act 1980, ss. 37 and 38).

Committal Proceedings

Procedure adopted at committal; reporting restrictions; bail; legal aid at committal; voluntary bills of indictment; notices of transfer under Criminal Justice Act 1987 (serious fraud) and Criminal Justice Act 1991 (child witnesses).

Juveniles and the Courts

Who is a juvenile; the work of the youth court; which courts can try juveniles; which courts can pass sentence on juveniles; limits on sentencing powers; committals for trial or sentence; publicity and public access; use of cautions by police.

Appeals from the Magistrates' Court

Appeals to the Crown Court; applications to the Divisional Court for judicial review or appeals by way of case stated; appeal to the House of Lords from the Divisional Court.

Indictments, Pleas and Crown Court Preliminaries

The structure of an indictment; separate counts and duplicity; joining several counts and accused in one indictment; amending indictments; use of alternative counts; pleas by the accused; fitness to plead; change of plea; plea to an alternative offence; abuse of process.

Crown Court: Pre-trial Issues

Disclosure; preparatory hearings; pre-trial hearings; plea and directions hearings.

Jury Trials

The sequence of a jury trial; absence of accused from court; when opening or closing speeches may be made; seeing the judge about plea or sentence; empanelling a jury; procedure where admissibility of evidence is disputed; making a formal admission; submission of no case to answer; alibi evidence; expert evidence; functions of judge and jury; contents of a summing-up; directions to a jury after their retirement; discharge of jurors; the verdict of the jury; majority verdicts; verdict of guilty of an alternative offence.

Appeals to the Court of Appeal

Certificate from the trial judge; getting leave to appeal from a single judge of the Court of Appeal; grounds of appeal against conviction – Criminal Appeal Act 1968, s. 2; appeal against sentence; appeals on fresh evidence; powers of the single judge; powers of the Court of Appeal; directions for loss of time; appeal to the House of Lords; reference to the European Court of Justice.

Sentencing and Costs

Basic sentencing powers of the Magistrates' and Crown Courts; sentencing procedure in both the Magistrates' and Crown Court; statutory principles and guidelines cases; maximum and minimum for common types of sentence or order; when such sentences or orders can be used; costs orders.

EVIDENCE SYLLABUS

Facts open to proof or disproof. Formal Admissions. Judicial Notice. Basic concepts: relevance, admissibility, weight and sufficiency.
Varieties of evidence.
Discretion.
Functions of judge and jury.
Burden and Standard of proof.
Presumptions (including conflicting presumptions, but in outline only).
Witnesses: attendance of witnesses and procedural issues, sworn and unsworn evidence and competence and compellability.
Examination-in-chief including leading questions, refreshing memory, previous consistent statements and unfavourable and hostile witnesses.
Cross-examination including liability to cross-examination, cross-examination on documents, cross-examination as to credit, the character of the complainant on charges of rape, previous inconsistent statements, and the rule of finality of answers to collateral questions and exceptions thereto.
Re-examination.
Similar fact evidence.
Character evidence.
The hearsay rule including its scope, original evidence, implied assertions, negative hearsay and statements produced by calculators etc.
Statutory and common-law exceptions to the hearsay rule.
Confessions including all relevant sections of the Police and Criminal Evidence Act 1984 and the Codes of Practice.
Illegally and improperly obtained evidence.
Inferences from accused's conduct, lies, failure to comply with the duty of disclosure, silence, failure or refusal to account for objects, substances, marks or presence at a particular place and refusal to consent to the taking of samples.
Opinion evidence including the relevant Crown Court Rules.
Judgments as evidence of the facts on which they are based including exceptions to the rule in *Hollington* v *Hewthorn*, convictions of the accused and convictions of persons other than the accused.
Corroboration and warnings required as a matter of practice.
Identification.
Privilege including privacy and confidential relationships.
Public interest immunity.
Documentary evidence.
Real evidence.

CIVIL MCT
ANSWER SHEET

Read the instructions before you start to fill in the answers.

INSTRUCTIONS

1. Use the HB pencil provided.
2. Fill in the boxes like this ■ not like this ☒ ✓
3. Fill in the boxes to indicate the subjects and whether this is a resit.
4. Write in your candidate number and the examination date in the spaces provided **and** fill in the boxes below.
5. Write your name and signature in the spaces provided.
6. Each question has four possible answers lettered A to D. Read all four answers **in full** before making a selection. Select the answer which you think is correct/best and indicate it on the answer sheet by filling in the appropriate box.
7. If you fill in 2 or more boxes in any question, that question will carry no mark.
8. Erase all mistakes thoroughly using the eraser provided.

CANDIDATE NUMBER

[0]	[0]	[0]	[0]
[1]	[1]	[1]	[1]
[2]	[2]	[2]	[2]
[3]	[3]	[3]	[3]
[4]	[4]	[4]	[4]
[5]	[5]	[5]	[5]
[6]	[6]	[6]	[6]
[7]	[7]	[7]	[7]
[8]	[8]	[8]	[8]
[9]	[9]	[9]	[9]

DATE OF EXAM
DAY   MONTH   YEAR

[0]	[0]	[0]	[0]
[1]	[1]	[1]	[1]
[2]	[2]	[2]	[2]
[3]	[3]	[3]	[3]
[4]	[4]	[4]	[4]
[5]	[5]	[5]	[5]
[6]	[6]	[6]	[6]
[7]	[7]	[7]	[7]
[8]	[8]	[8]	[8]
[9]	[9]	[9]	[9]

SUBJECT

Evidence & Civil Litigation [ ]   [ ]

Evidence & Criminal Litigation   [ ]

Is this a resit?   Yes [ ]
                   No [ ]

CRIMINAL MCT
ANSWER SHEET

Read the instructions before you start to fill in the answers.

INSTRUCTIONS

1. Use the HB pencil provided.
2. Fill in the boxes like this ▬ not like this ☒ ✓
3. Fill in the boxes to indicate the subjects and whether this is a resit.
4. Write in your candidate number and the examination date in the spaces provided **and** fill in the boxes below.
5. Write your name and signature in the spaces provided.
6. Each question has four possible answers lettered A to D. Read all four answers **in full** before making a selection. Select the answer which you think is correct/best and indicate it on the answer sheet by filling in the appropriate box.
7. If you fill in 2 or more boxes in any question, that question will carry no mark.
8. Erase all mistakes thoroughly using the eraser provided.

SUBJECT

Evidence & Civil Litigation [ ]

Evidence & Criminal Litigation [ ]

Is this a resit? Yes [ ] No [ ]

CANDIDATE NUMBER

[0]	[0]	[0]	[0]
[1]	[1]	[1]	[1]
[2]	[2]	[2]	[2]
[3]	[3]	[3]	[3]
[4]	[4]	[4]	[4]
[5]	[5]	[5]	[5]
[6]	[6]	[6]	[6]
[7]	[7]	[7]	[7]
[8]	[8]	[8]	[8]
[9]	[9]	[9]	[9]

DATE OF EXAM
DAY MONTH YEAR

[0]	[0]	[0]	[0]
[1]	[1]	[1]	[1]
[2]	[2]	[2]	[2]
[3]	[3]	[3]	[3]
[4]	[4]	[4]	[4]
[5]	[5]	[5]	[5]
[6]	[6]	[6]	[6]
[7]	[7]	[7]	[7]
[8]	[8]	[8]	[8]
[9]	[9]	[9]	[9]